Liz –
So wonderful to connect with
you at LCLC2016.
Enjoy the world of women's
basketball!
Cheers,

Why She Plays

The World of Women's Basketball

Christine A. Baker   *Foreword by Becky Hammon*

UNIVERSITY OF NEBRASKA PRESS ● LINCOLN AND LONDON

Library of Congress
Cataloging-in-Publication Data
Baker, Christine A.
Why she plays: the world of
women's basketball / Christine A.
Baker; foreword by Becky Hammon.
p.   cm.
Includes bibliographical references.
ISBN 978-0-8032-1633-4
(pbk.: alk. paper)
1. Basketball for women—United
States—History. 2. Women basketball players—United States—Biography. 3. Basketball players—United
States—Biography. [1. Basketball for
women—History.] I. Title.
GV886.B29   2008
796.323'8—dc22
2008027794

Set in Swift EF by Bob Reitz.
Designed by A. Shahan.

For the players.

Why I Play

When there is turmoil and questions
here, I find silence.
When there is pain and wonder
here, I find solitude.
When there is joy
here, I find space.

Just one simple rim
out in nowhere
up in the clouds
in a quiet gym

a 'lil slice of beauty,

doesn't have to be pristine
with nets beautifying the edge
doesn't have to have lights and fans
surrounding the post
just give me a rim and there I'll be
anywhere, any place
a place to be . . . me
the most.

It's a simple thing,
just put the ball in the rim
the movement, the dance
believe and it goes in,
miss and try again
win, lose, enjoy
life.

That's why I play.

Jacquie Shackelford

Contents

Foreword   xi

Acknowledgments   xv

Introduction: Why She Plays   1

PART ONE   YOUTH BASKETBALL

1   Heck Yeah, I'm a Tomboy!   9

2   The Fun Factor   16

PART TWO   HIGH-SCHOOL BASKETBALL

3   You Can't Measure Heart   33

4   The Crème of the Crop   42

PART THREE   COLLEGE BASKETBALL

5   Three Divisions, One Association   55

6   Conradt, Goestenkors, and the
    Pursuit of Perfection   65

7   The Approach of a Coach   75

8   A Dance Is Still a Dance   89

PART FOUR   THE WNBA

9   Over Ten Years and Going Strong
    in the WNBA   99

10   The Superstars and the "Special"
     Treatment   112

PART FIVE   USA BASKETBALL

11   The United States versus the
     Rest of the World   125

12   The Best in the World   131

PART SIX   MEDIA COVERAGE AND
           WOMEN'S BASKETBALL

13   The Slippery Slope of Gender
     Politics   147

14   Unique but Alike   158

15   Her Place of Peace   170

     Epilogue: Building the Perfect
     Player   181

     Appendix A: High School
     Participation by State   187

     Appendix B: The Structure of
     USA Basketball   189

     Notes   193

     Suggested Reading   197

Foreword Becky Hammon

Listening to howling coyotes and sitting underneath the big sky and millions of stars were things I did often growing up in South Dakota. I remember admiring the works of an awesome Creator, not realizing what plans He had for my life. It was difficult for me to comprehend how all those millions of stars were hung.

At night after the floodlights were turned off on our concrete basketball court and my brother and father had gone in the house, I would routinely stand out there on the darkened basketball court, dreaming. Often I would let my thoughts run wild and imagine hitting game winners, buzzer beaters, circus shots, and nailing daggers from twenty-five feet out. Imagination aside, I could not foresee how my life and career would connect in the world of women's basketball.

Growing up in South Dakota, I was shielded from the recruiting craziness that now accompanies any girl who is a great high-school basketball player. I have considered that a blessing and always will. It's one of the most basic and pure beliefs about life in America: No handouts, just good ole fashioned hard work! America is about opportunities. If there is (and I believe there is) an American dream for a women's basketball player, I'm living proof of that dream come true. All I asked for was a fair opportunity, and I received it.

I do believe that any girl from any state, at any age, who picks up a basketball and has a dream, does so because it is fun. Dreams unify us and anchor our hearts together. Everyone may have dreams, but few chase them, and even fewer are blessed to live them.

For me that dreaming was fun. The countless hours I spent alone in the gym were fun. On that court I developed my passion and love for the game of basketball along with my desire to improve myself each and every day. That's the reason why I played and fell in love with this beautiful game.

I play this game for many reasons now, not simply because I love it. I play it to inspire the 99 percent of people who are told they aren't good enough, tall enough, or didn't come from the "right program." I play it because I love giving a high-five to a little girl or boy who will never forget that moment and won't wash their hands for the next week. I play because I want to give you that precise moment that made your heart skip a beat and made you leap out of your seat. I play because I want to see you scratch your head and wonder how in the heck I made that shot into the basket. I play because of the BIGGER picture! I play because every time I walk out onto the court I have the opportunity to blaze a trail through the minds of men, women, boys, and girls and show by example that we should judge an athlete not by the contour of their physique but by the character by which they compete. I play to honor those women who came before me who blazed a trail for me to have this singular opportunity. I play because I love destroying every stereotype, every cultural and gender barrier that our society argues doesn't exist anymore. I play so that every mother, sister, daughter, or niece can walk into any job interview or situation in life and be given a fair opportunity. I play because every female and male needs to see and understand what a confident, informed, inspired, and qualified woman can do when she puts her mind to something. I play to inspire you to dream bigger than you think you can and to climb higher than what you've been told is safe. I play basketball because it reminds me that no matter what people say I can't do, God says I can.

If all these reasons were taken away and there were no more dreams to be dreamed, no more minds to be opened, or people to be entertained and inspired, I'd still step out onto my old basketball court in South Dakota. I'd play until it was dark out, turn on the floodlights, and play some more. I'd play just because it's fun, and the court is where I love to be.

Acknowledgments

Writing a book about basketball is nearly impossible without accessing and utilizing a variety of statistics. In many cases these statistics help paint the picture of a particular player, coach, or program. Please note that the statistics given throughout this text were current as of June 2007.

I would like to thank the many people who helped me with this project: authors Paul Krafin and Catherine Whitney for their generosity, faith, and stubborn insistence that this story was worth telling; Clay Kallam at *Full Court Press* for his knowledge of the WNBA and willingness to show me the ropes; Becky Hammon for graciously taking the time to share her thoughts and time; special thanks to the WNBA, NCAA, Women's Sports Foundation, and National Federation of State High School Associations for sharing a wealth of information; Caroline Williams from USA Basketball and Ron Howard from the WNBA for their assistance and patience; Val Ackerman and Donna Lopiano for their time; Christopher Dougherty for coming through in the clutch; Dr. Indira Karamcheti from Wesleyan University; special thanks to all the players and coaches who generously donated their time and thoughts to help make this book real; my fellow masterminds for their unwavering support and inspiration; Dara Onofrio for being my friend, angel, and toughest critic; and finally to my parents and grandparents—the four corners of my world.

Portions of this book originally appeared, often in different form, as the following:

"Life with the Liberty: A Bittersweet Journey: What Might Have Been, What Might Be," *Full Court Press*, June 15, 2005, http://www.full court.com. Reprinted courtesy of *Full Court Press*.

"Life with the Liberty: Dreams Battle with Reality: Basketball Goes One-on-One with Life," *Full Court Press*, August 22, 2005, http://www.fullcourt.com. Reprinted courtesy of *Full Court Press*.

"Place of Peace," *Confluence: The Journal of Graduate Liberal Studies* 12, no. 2 (Spring 2007): 50–57.

"Ticha and 'Kesha Tell All: Key Players from the WNBA's Best Teams Are Hungry for a Title," *Full Court Press*, September 1, 2005, http://www.fullcourt.com. Reprinted courtesy of *Full Court Press*.

"You Can't Measure Heart," *Got Game Magazine*, Summer 2005, 16.

Why She Plays

Sports do not build character. They reveal it. HAYWOOD HALE BROUN

Introduction Why She Plays

One Friday night in July 2005, I walked out of the tunnel and onto the floor of Madison Square Garden moments before the New York Liberty basketball team did the same. I was aware of the lights behind me flipping on to illuminate the way for the players and the television cameras. I saw the electrical wires crisscrossing down the tunnel and underneath the hardwood floor. Only steps ahead of the team, I watched the fans look beyond me to the players they had paid to see. There was fanfare. There was noise, but it was not for me and it never will be. I am like a ghost forever hovering at the edges of the tunnel, riding the shadows of the players, trying to grasp the ball as it slips just out of reach of my fingertips.

Over 99 percent of all basketball players never have the opportunity to play professionally, and I am one of the majority. Nevertheless, since my father bought me my first basketball at the age of six, I dreamed of being a superstar. Twenty-eight years later, not much has changed. Some nights when sleep eludes me, I hear the sold-out arena chant my name, "Bak-er, Bak-er." The voices collectively urge me toward that sacred place of glory I still vividly envision.

Sadly the reality is that a sold-out arena will never chant my name. An Olympic gold medal will never be gently placed over my bowed head. Not every one of us is chosen for Olympic glory. Legions of quiet superstars play because we want to. We work against the odds of height or build or natural ability because we want to better ourselves, because we have a profound love of a game. We have, each one of us, those moments to treasure after practice in the empty gym. Those hours after dark in the playgrounds and backyards across America are ours and ours alone.

I might never be a professional basketball player, but the court will forever be my home. Basketball is in my blood. It's in my heart. I play because I love the sound of a leather ball slipping elusively through a chain net. I love the cracks in a blacktop court where the weeds poke through. I love the sound sneakers make on a shiny indoor court. I love the competition and the camaraderie. That's why I play. Why do you?

My father gave me my first basketball and hoop in the summer of 1980 when I was six years old. I recall the orange basketball nestled among countless stuffed animals on my bed, waiting, pleading for me to pick it up and make it a part of me. I was born an only child in rural Connecticut, but when I saw that ball, I found my twin, my parallel soul. It was instantaneous, a connection so powerful that to this day, I marvel at its intensity and longevity.

It didn't take me long to get hooked. I watched basketball on television well past my bedtime. I slept with the ball, walked around the neighborhood with the ball, did everything with that ball. Early on, my tutors were Larry Bird, Magic Johnson, and Julius Erving. It was absolute enchantment to watch Dr. J hit a swinging, graceful jump hook on television, but it was pure bliss to practice hook shots and fadeaway jumpers in my driveway until well past dark. I believed then with every fiber of my being that I was meant to play basketball—nothing more and nothing less.

I vividly recall watching the 1984 NBA Finals with my mom and dad in our family room on a big black Naugahyde couch. My beloved Boston Celtics, the blue-collar team made up of Larry Bird, Robert Parish, Danny Ainge, Dennis Johnson, and Kevin McHale against the Hollywood glitter of the Lost Angeles Lakers, led by Magic Johnson, along with Kareem Abdul-Jabbar, James Worthy, Byron Scott, and the rough Kurt Rambis. It was patience versus running, East versus West, tradition versus glamour. It was a brutal series, one that caused Lakers' head coach Pat Riley to lose his legendary cool more than once. The games began late, and I was up until well past midnight clutching a pillow to my face as the action on the court became too intense.

The '84 Celtics weren't physically imposing or flashy. They were smart and relentless, and Larry Bird epitomized this persona. The skinny red head from French Lick, Indiana, did things with a basketball that made the hair on my arms stand on end. He wasn't a vocal leader, but he led his team by example, and they followed. Hell, I followed, and I was only an eleven-year-old girl. Larry Bird led that team not with an outspoken demeanor but with his play. He let his game do the talking. His teammates, and I, listened well.

For a girl in the early 1980s, it just wasn't that simple. While there were plenty of winter basketball leagues and summer basketball camps, they were for boys, not girls. I played on boys basketball teams with Lions Club in Haddam, Connecticut. Because I was one of the best players in the league, the other boys didn't make much of the fact that I played. I recall only one other girl who played with me. We were never on the same team, but I remember she was good. She was tall and wore long, colorful ribbons attached to her barrettes.

It wasn't until 1983 that an all-girls league began in my hometown. When the girls' league began, she switched over, as did I. We were the only two girls who had been good enough to hold our own with the boys, so whenever we faced one another, we were both extremely motivated. On those rare occasions we stared one another down at the start of the game in a way that would make Mohammad Ali proud. Barrettes or no barrettes, ribbons or no ribbons, we were primed for battle. I don't recall who outplayed the other in those early games, but I do remember the level of intensity and the fierce competitiveness we both brought to the court. I often wonder what became of her and if basketball is as much a part of her soul as it is mine.

When I was fifteen years old, in my diary I swore with the solemnity of a subpoenaed witness, with a tiny pin prick of blood to mark the spot, that I would never forget the sound of a chain net in the school playground or the way my hands had become molded to the round softness of a leather ball. I promised that I would play basketball forever. I promised all this because I thought I should make it official on the off chance things would change down the road.

That promise, however innocent and well intentioned, marked a turning point in my relationship to the game. By acknowledging my deep connection to the game, I twisted my relationship with it and forced upon it a value better left unmentioned. I imposed myself upon the game without its permission, and ultimately, I burned out. Through high school and college I felt the weight of its burden over its beauty, its struggle more than its solace. I grew to fear my obsession with improving.

When I graduated from college in 1995, I could no longer articulate my love for the game. Instead I was afraid it had swallowed me up, afraid I would never be good at anything else. As a result I ran as far from the game of basketball as I could. I worked on a career in publications management with the same intensity I had once worked on my jump shot. Simply I was determined to succeed without a ball in my hands.

One morning in February of 2005 I woke up to the cold gray sunrise and dressed for work. Before I left for the office, I looked at myself in the full-length mirror. Neatly dressed with dark slacks and a blue silk turtleneck, my blond hair pulled up off my face, I no longer recognized the person staring back at me. I stood, reflected in that mirror, alone—the court and the backboards were gone. The ball racks, sneakers, and water bottles — gone too. In their place was a briefcase filled with proofs and schedules, a Palm Pilot with names and appointments I could barely keep track of, and a cell phone with five unheard messages. I had allowed myself to walk away from the game I loved. I had misled myself, and the hurt finally hit me. As I inhaled, I felt the air rattle around my hollow insides, and I realized that like the Grinch, my heart had grown three sizes too small.

Determined to make a change, I walked away from a career as a publications director. I walked away from routine and direct deposit, good benefits and stability that would have easily led to a nice house at the end of a cul-de-sac, to find my way back to the game of basketball. I knew it was a leap of faith, but quite simply I wanted to go home.

Home became a pressroom in the underbelly of an arena. Home is listening to starting lineups and transcribing interviews. Home is writing for little or no money about the game I love. I'm not surprised anymore when sports editors tell me that my writing is good but that they can't afford to pay someone only to cover the WNBA.

I learned that the business of basketball is entertainment. I learned how difficult it is for women's sports to compete in the global marketplace. I talked with players at the highest level who struggle to maintain their individuality in a league that treats players as commodities (just as in any professional sports league), as products to be bought and sold in hopes of creating the magic formula that will win a championship.

Sometimes I fear that I've turned cynical about the world of women's basketball. Whenever that feeling becomes overwhelming, I just close my eyes and think back to Teresa Weatherspoon with her fists raised high at the Garden after she hit that amazing fifty-foot buzzer beater on September 4, 1999, in Game 2 of the WNBA finals against Houston. I think back to the high-school team I coach and the joy we experienced when one of my players hit a similar shot in a playoff game just last season.

When the business overwhelms me, I recall that unmistakable gym smell of sweat and hardwood and movement. Before I know it, I can hear the game again—sneakers squeaking on the hardwood, bodies flying down the court, players calling picks—I can feel the precise choreography and that gossamer-thin connection between players and ball, and then it's all OK, and it's all worth it, lousy paycheck and all.

Acclaimed sports writer Steve Wilstein once said, "Nobody cares how much effort it takes or what you have to do to get the story in, just as long as you do." While that statement is true, there are still some of us out there who write about the sport not just to turn in a story but also to feel connected once more to the game we love so much.

Part one Youth Basketball

1 Heck Yeah, I'm a Tomboy!

The wide aisle swallowed me, and I immediately imagined heaven must look like this: rows of aluminum bats, all different sizes; volleyball nets; footballs; helmets in every color; batting gloves; golf clubs; things to throw; things to catch.

No one else was shopping in that particular aisle of Bradlees in Middletown, Connecticut. It must've been a Saturday because Mom always did her errands and shopping on Saturdays. I was eight or nine years old. Mom was in the next aisle looking for tea sets or Barbie dolls—something feminine and pretty for her daughter to play with—but the moment I spotted the Barbie doll with the glazed eyes and painted smile sitting stiffly in a pink box, I felt sick. Who needed a Barbie doll when I could dress up my Siamese cat, Charlie, instead? What I really needed was that football helmet.

Moments before mom pulled me out of Bradlees, disappointed in my lack of interest in the Barbie doll or the tea set, she saw someone she knew and stopped to talk. I seized my opportunity and went back to the sporting-goods aisle. I strapped on a blue and red New York Giants helmet and dribbled a basketball. Within seconds an imaginary game with imaginary rules, goal lines, and two distinctly different teams had begun. Of course I scored the winning point in the last second of the game. If by chance I missed once or twice, I must have been fouled.

Right in the middle of my celebration dance, a young boy and his father walked onto my imaginary field. How rude, I thought. The father had his hand on the kid's shoulder, and I remember that the little boy had freckles and red hair just like his dad's.

The helmet was a few sizes too big, and I had trouble seeing, so I pulled it off my head. My long blond hair spilled out from inside the helmet. With the helmet on I was just another kid. With the helmet off I was a girl—a girl in the sports aisle of Bradlees. The little boy poked his father in the side and laughed loud. He said to me, "Hey Blondie, you're in the wrong aisle. Dolls are in the girls' aisle over there. What are you, a tomboy?"

The dad smirked. The son smirked. I stood dumbly staring at the boy and his father. I didn't quite know what to do. I couldn't really put the helmet back on and continue playing. I stood there with my cheeks flushed deep red and a Giants football helmet hanging loosely at my side, embarrassed about something I did not entirely understand.

In that moment a feeling of inferiority eclipsed the sheer joy of winning my imaginary game, and it made me both confused and angry. It had never occurred to me that my love of sports, the catches in the backyard with my dad or the random game of P-I-G on the basketball court were wrong or even unusual. I could not fathom that playing sports, for anyone, could be a problem.

My mom finished talking and walked over to me. The boy and his dad were gone, but I still stood in the same spot and stared down at my red Converse sneakers with tears streaming down my face. She bent down and quietly wiped the tears from my cheek and asked why I was crying.

"They called me a tomboy. I don't even know what that means, but it must be a bad word because of how they said it," I recall sobbing into her soft embrace. To her credit mom told me not to worry about what other people thought and bought me that Giants helmet.

I was called a tomboy quite a bit in the coming years. When I played in the Lions Club boys' Youth League, I'd hear opponents and even parents of the opponents whispering it to one another like I had leprosy or the plague, but the boys who were my teammates thought nothing of it, and neither did the coaches.

I still remember my first two coaches in the Lions Club Youth League. Other than my dad, they were my first true teachers of the game. Coach P. was a stout, no-nonsense police officer named Phil Pessina, who had a mustache like Tom Selleck's. Coach Sipples had scraggly blond hair and long sideburns but knew the game extremely well. They both treated me exactly the same as every other player on their team, an important nondistinction in a time when little girls still weren't entirely welcome playing sports. Coach P. and Coach Sipples taught me how to shoot a proper jump shot. They taught me how to use my body to draw contact on a drive, how to take a charge, how to box out. They taught me no differently than they did the boys. In order to prove to them that I was worthy of their confidence, I played hard and practiced harder.

Because the coaches treated me like any other player on the team, my teammates did the same. They acted as if they possessed a secret weapon. Usually during a timeout, one of them, a boy named Matt with dark black hair and serious eyes, would usually say something like, "ok, Baker. Did you hear number eight call you a tomboy? Did you hear it, boys? Let's show him what happens when you mess with us." Confidently I knew that "us" included me. We'd high-five out of the timeout, and inevitably I'd wind up with the ball. It was my sole job to attack number eight, or number four, or whoever the poor little soul was that thought it a good idea to make fun of me. Both my parents lost count of how many boys I made cry. Mom smiled proudly at the parents of those boys who would plead with her to make it stop. One mother said, "Please, Sylvia. Tell her to take it easy on him. He'll be crying for the next three days, and we have a birthday party after this."

First Memories

Tamika Catchings, Olympian and All-Star forward for the Indiana Fever, like me, was called a tomboy, although she never recalls feeling uncomfortable by the title. The former University of Tennessee standout said, "Heck yeah, I was called a tomboy all the time, but to me, that was a good thing. I was proud to be a tomboy." Catchings's goal growing up was to play professional basketball, and a nickname wasn't going to stop her. "I worked really hard to reach that goal, starting from an early age. It was all I really ever wanted to do," she said.

Diana Taurasi, Olympian and All-Star guard for the Phoenix Mercury has become the face of the WNBA and arguably of USA Basketball. Not only did Taurasi lead UConn to three consecutive national championships, she one of only three other players to win the Naismith Player of the Year Award in back-to-back seasons. Always outspoken Taurasi has a contagious energy when she talks about the game. She said, "My first memory was playing for the Cheeno Cheetahs. We had bright yellow and orange uniforms. We practiced outside, and we always played against the boys. Those are the memories I'll always keep." By eighth grade, Taurasi realized that she was both good at basketball and interested in improving: "I don't know if I was better than anyone at the time, but I picked up skills faster than anyone else. It was always a game I just loved to play."

Cara Murphy, a former player at Fairfield University, might not have a trophy case as large as Taurasi's, but her first basketball memories are equally powerful. She remembered playing the game as second grader in a local recreation league. She also played regularly with her father, who also played basketball in college. "Dad and I would walk down the street to a little elementary-school park, and we would play. Even when I couldn't reach the basket, he would pick me up and try to teach me how to shoot," said Murphy. She has a younger sister who also plays basketball: "We were really competitive. I'd always try to show her up, but now she's a great player in her own right."

Crystal Robinson, longtime WNBA player turned assistant coach for the Washington Mystics, laughed as she recalled her first memories with a basketball: "Both of my parents are basketball players, and it was just something that was natural to me. My dad put a basketball in my hands when I was four or five years old. I remember I had a Nerf goal, and I broke it dunkin' on it all the time. Basketball just came easy to me. My dad played me one-on-one a lot, but he didn't really push me to play. My cousins were my role models. I used to watch them play basketball. They were really good, and I wanted to be like them. We always played around my house. The only thing I can remember wanting to do was beat my cousin Kevin. My biggest goal in life was to beat him." Robinson didn't skip a beat. She laughed and finished with, "I beat him several times as I got older."

Fun Is the Name of the Game

Thirty-six years have passed since the 1972 enactment of Title IX, a federal law prohibiting sex discrimination in federally funded education, including athletics. Large numbers of girls and women have benefited from this legislation by way of increased athletic opportunities and equal facilities. The experience I had as a child in the late '70s is vastly different than the experiences of Diana Taurasi or Cara Murphy. Girls leagues were becoming prevalent, and parents no longer adhered to the mindset that girls could not play sports. By the mid to late '80s, it didn't matter if you were a girl. What mattered was if you could play.

Simply, the landscape is no longer the same as it was in 1979—or in 1989 even. Researchers and sports psychologists continue to write books and conduct studies about how society's views of female athletes have or have not changed since the introduction of Title IX. Many arguments continue, but for the young female athletes themselves, playing basketball has become one of many realistic and recognized options. Without Title IX there may never have been a Diana Taurasi or a Becky Hammon.

The passage of Title IX has had, and continues to have, a tremendous impact in terms of participation. According to a 2000

Women's Sports Foundation press release, in the year prior to the passage of the law, "only one in 27 school girls participated in varsity sports. In 1998, that figure was an astounding one in three—nearly equal to the figure for male sports participation, which was one in two."[1]

In 1999 slightly over 12 million females age six and over played basketball, a 15 percent increase over the 11 million in 1987, the first year the study was conducted. Additionally girls compose 44 percent of all organized sports team members.[2] About 80 percent of women identified as key leaders in Fortune 500 companies participated in sports during their childhood and self-identified as having been "tomboys."[3]

On the downside according to the Centers for Disease Control and Prevention, almost half of America's youth do not take part in regular vigorous exercise. Fourteen percent of youths report no physical activity at all.[4] Donna Lopiano, former CEO of the Women's Sports Foundation is an outspoken leader in the cause of preventing youth obesity. She said, "We're confronting a real obesity and health crisis that will translate into one out of every three children born in the year 2000 contracting Type II Diabetes. This is a real emphasis for us. We're working to get one million sedentary girls active."

Dr. Dan Gould, director of the Institute for the Study of Youth Sports (ISYS) at Michigan State University is a sport psychology specialist and coaching educator. He studies stress, burnout, and motivation in young athletes, how high-school coaches teach life skills to their players, talent development in children, and the role that parents play in youth sports. He is best known for his efforts to link sport science research to practice and practice back to research.

Dr. Gould believes it's vital for parents to understand that youth sports is about having fun and developing healthy habits, not about preparing a child for a career in professional sports. The mission of the ISYS is to provide leadership, conduct scientific research, and engage in service or outreach that transforms the face of youth sports in ways that maximize the beneficial physical, psychological, and social effects of participation for children and youth while minimizing detrimental effects. ISYS was launched in 1978 after members of the Michigan legislature became concerned about negative and unhealthy practices in youth sports.

According to Dr. Gould, children have multiple reasons for playing sports: to be with their friends, to have a good time, to get good at something and learn skills, and to feel confident. Sometimes social evaluation creates too much pressure at too early an age. "Kids feel stress and pressure. Stress research shows that once children feel pressured as a result of being evaluated by adults, or they feel they are going to fail, then their enjoyment potentially decreases," said Dr. Gould.

He believes that part of the problem is the so-called professionalization of children's sports, or, as Dr. Gould suggests, the "Venus Williams/Tiger Woods effect": "Parents apply pressure by believing their child will be a star tennis or basketball player at four years old." He urges parents to ask themselves if they are letting their child choose her interest rather than choosing it for her. He suggests that parents expose a child to multiple sports and allow her to fall in love with one. If she's lucky enough to have some talent, then she should pursue the sport from there. "There is a role for healthy competition, but as sport scientists we are worried it starts too early," said Dr. Gould.

Dr. Gould regularly asks parents of young athletes a simple question: If you are lucky enough to have a little girl who wants to play sports, what do you really want her to get out of it? The primary reasons for children to play sports is to be physically active, to learn life skills, to have fun, to be with her friends, and to have a successful winning experience. "Sure, winning is part of it, but at the youth level, it's not about winning. It's about learning how to work with kids she doesn't like. It's about developing a lifelong habit of physical activity so she doesn't have osteoporosis when she is eighty. These are the reasons why young girls should play basketball," said Dr. Gould.

Young girls also might play basketball for the bright orange and yellow uniforms, as Diana Taurasi recalled. Some of us are magnetically pulled toward the game, and once we get a taste of it, we're hooked for life, cool uniforms or not.

2 The Fun Factor

Coaching youth basketball is a little bit like trying to catch lightning in a bottle. I learned this while coaching peewee basketball several years ago. There is no teaching help defense or crossover dribbles in peewee basketball. I spent two hours a week teaching them which direction the ball and their bodies needed to go. My eyes welled up when one of them dribbled without hitting her forehead with the ball. I was ecstatic when five little girls would slap their tiny hands on the floor before playing a defense they had no idea how to do correctly. Hell, I was excited if the girls shot at the correct basket. The parents were excited that I was willing to work with their kids. Even though Title IX is thirty-six years old, not many young women have become involved in coaching youth sports. When one of us volunteers our time, we tend to stick out. The recreation director was thrilled that I wanted to volunteer my time as a youth coach because according to him, "We don't see too many young women wanting to help out in this way."

The parents of the kids I coached sent me cards and flowers, Christmas gifts and poems. They made the experience so positive for me. Reaching those children returned far more to me than I had taught them. Parent after parent made it a point to tell me how important it was for their daughter to have a young woman as a role model. That being said, I have noticed a dramatic difference in the girls who play youth sports. When I played, I knew I was different. I worked extra hard to prove my worth, to make sure I could keep playing. Now young girls play basketball in their own leagues because they want to, without the added pressure of constant comparison to boys. If they like it, they continue. If not, they move on to a different experience. That's how it should be.

Shay is eight years old and lives in a small shoreline town in Connecticut. She likes to play basketball, but for her it's just another activity that's fun. Because she's small, she can sneak around and between people's legs and steal the ball. Sometimes the boys and girls play basketball together in gym class. She practices every day in her driveway with her older brother, who helps her shoot and is teaching her the game. Shay told me quickly, "I don't like shooting because I'm too short. Every time I shoot, I miss. Right now, I like to steal the ball. My brother and I are a good team. I just want to play to have fun. If I start shooting like Diana Taurasi, then I'll play when I'm older. Diana is my favorite player because she's very good at basketball. She works really hard. When Diana retires she's gonna want to be my best friend."

I asked Shay what other professional athletes she knows. After careful consideration and conferring quickly with her mom, Shay responded, "Derek Jeter with the Yankees. LeBron James because he has a cool gum commercial. I like Michael Jordan. I never saw him play, but I know he's a good player. I know him from TV. He did that slam dunk with his arm way up in the air."

Finally I asked Shay if she ever wanted to play in the WNBA. She thought for a moment while picking at a hole in her jeans. "I like it, but I don't know if I'm good enough. I like sports. I want to be a doctor, a ballerina, and a mommy. I like softball and soccer. Basketball takes hard work. I don't know if I'm good enough."

Kristin from New York is eleven years old. She's much different from Shay in her desire to play basketball. For Kristin it's not just about participating or spending time with her older brother. Simply she is an eleven-year-old girl in love with the game. On a typical weekend Kristin spends hours on the playground shooting baskets. She'll play with her family, or she'll play pickup ball with the kids from the neighborhood.

Because of Kristin's interest in the sport, I've taken her to some practices with the high-school team I coach at Rye Country Day School. The first practice she attended, Kristin spent the first thirty minutes facing the wall, too shy to turn around. After an hour she came out of her shell and dribbled around on her own. By the end of practice, one of my players said to me, "Hey Coach, that kid is better than I am!"

Kristin sat on the bench during a few of our games, filling water bottles, picking up empty cups. She proudly wore her Wildcats Basketball T-shirt, and I noticed how quickly, even though she was shy, she picked up basic skills and techniques of the game. In fact I wish some of my high-school players picked things up like she did.

One chilly morning on the way to practice, Kristin's love of basketball spilled out in a measured and clear manner. As we crossed the Hudson River on the Tappan Zee Bridge, Kristin told me the first time she started playing basketball was in kindergarten: "I remember after school, I would hurry to finish my homework so I could play basketball." She paused, her hands folded in her lap, her eyes on the window of my Saab, as if speaking to the window made her forget she was saying any of this out loud. Kristin said, "I like that when you shoot it can go in. I like watching three pointers. Michael Jordan and Becky Hammon are my favorite players. I saw Becky play last year. I liked being there because you can see how far they can shoot and how fast they play. I like softball, tennis, and soccer, but I like basketball the best. I'm sometimes afraid to play with the boys, but I do it anyway."

I asked her a simple question: When you go to sleep at night and you dream of when you're grown up, what do you dream? She thought for a moment and said barely loud enough for me to hear, "I dream that I'm gonna be a star basketball player and be in the WNBA and sign autographs."

"Me too," I said. "I still fall asleep at night dreaming the very same thing."

"But you can't," Kristin replied. "You're too old."

"Yes, but I was once your age, and I loved basketball the way you do now."

When I was eleven, a very tall man and his wife visited my parents at our rural home in Higganum, Connecticut. As an only child, I learned quickly how to talk with adults and feel comfortable in their presence, but this visit was different. The tall man kept smiling at me and winking to my dad. Unbeknownst to me, my father had invited an old friend over to help assess my talent for and my seriousness about basketball. Everyone was in on the secret except me.

Bored and restless, I left the living room to find something else to occupy my time. Without so much as a pause, I grabbed the ball from the bottom step of the garage landing, dribbling between the cars in the garage out to the driveway. Dad had recently put up a new hoop over the garage doors, and he had even painted a foul line for me.

It was a muggy and warm early June evening. I took my dog, Sam, a big protective black lab, outside with me. After about twenty minutes, I was sweaty and entirely in my own world. Daily, before he left for his second-shift job at Pratt and Whitney Aircraft, Dad instructed me how keep my elbow in and bend my knees when I shot the ball. During the NBA season, we watched games together, and he pointed out the proper footwork to post up, or the proper way to shoot a foul shot. Then, when I was alone, I tried to relive those moments and practice what my dad had shown me.

I was so intently focused on my own personal instruction I

didn't notice the tall man leaned up against the garage entrance watching me. "Mind if I shoot around with you? I need to stretch out these creaky bones," he said.

"Nope, I don't mind. Here," I answered, tossing him the ball and trying not to look surprised. Even at this age, I had mastered the cardinal rule of basketball: the art of nonchalance. If you're scared, it's imperative you look calm and serene. If you are unsure of your abilities, you've got to seem nonplussed or you're dead. My face was devoid of any emotion, but inside, my stomach was doing flips.

He didn't miss. Not once. Over and over again. Swish. Swish. He dribbled effortlessly between his long legs, behind his back, with one hand, faster than I could imagine anyone dribbling. I forgot about his height, enthralled with the way his body moved as one with the ball.

"Play a little defense on me, will ya, this is getting too easy," he shouted as he flew right by me.

I nodded, excited by the opportunity to become involved in his dialogue with the ball. He quickly chimed in "winner's outs," before I had a chance to argue. With that an unlikely one-on-one game began. In the same way it's done in thousands of playgrounds and backyard hoops around the world, the offensive player faces the basket at the top of the key. The ball is "checked" or passed to the defender. The moment the defender (in this case, me) tosses the ball to the other person (the tall guy), the game is on. The term "winner's out" means that the person who scores continues to play offense until he or she misses a shot.

He began dribbling super slow and high, keeping the ball at eye level for me. "Well, go ahead, steal it," he joked.

"OK," I said as I swiped at the ball, certain I could steal it. I never got a clean look at the ball again until it went through the hoop. He did that two more times. I was angry and remember thinking nobody should come to my house and beat me at my hoop. I picked up the effort level. I ran around, flailing my arms and sliding my feet on defense just trying to keep up.

My parents and his wife came outside to watch us play. Now I had fans. Loud fans. I tried every move I had—all two of them. I bumped him on defense and pushed against his legs. Somehow the ball slid loose and hit me in the knees. This was my moment to show him something special, something unexpected. He was so unbelievably tall. I crossed over quickly to my weaker right hand, slipped just out of reach of his long arm, and scored a right-handed lay-up. After I scored, I ran to my fans and high-fived each one like I had just won the NBA Championship at the buzzer.

"I'll tell you what, Vin," he said to my dad just loud enough for me to hear. "Look at her eyes. Do you see that? Did you see her while we played? She's got something. Sure she's coordinated and athletic. Keep working with her. She's got what you can't teach a kid. She's got fire."

I didn't know until many years later that the Boston Celtics had drafted the tall man several years before my first and only meeting with him. He had never played a professional game because he blew out his knee three weeks before the season started. Neither one of us ever saw our dreams become our realities. He never heard his name announced at the old Boston Garden, nor did I, but one summer day in June of 1984, we were an unlikely pair playing the same game that filled both of our hearts with joy. In those pure moments with my worn out basketball, a tall man and a little girl became inextricably linked together on a driveway basketball court with only the thin whisper of a ball through a backyard hoop and our sneakers on the pavement playing our favorite symphony.

The Gym Rat

Janelle, from Mount Vernon, New York, is an older version of Kristin, and reminds me a little of myself. She's a gym rat, and she possesses that fire that's nearly impossible to teach. At fifteen years old, Janelle is five feet three, with the heart of a six-foot center. We chose to bring her up to the varsity team at Rye Country Day School as a freshman because of her attitude and work ethic.

During the summer, I talked with Janelle about basketball. She was one of those eighth graders you couldn't keep out of the gym. Worn down by her persistence, I invited her to watch practices. By the end of the season, Janelle knew most of the plays better than the varsity team did.

Janelle told me she first began playing basketball when she was eight years old. "Basketball was always accessible where I lived in the North Bronx. I had four parks within walking distance from my home. Growing up with more male friends than female ones, it was how I bonded with many peers. My first memory in the game was my first steal and fast break in a pickup game with boys."

Once I asked Janelle if she was ever called a tomboy. She laughed. "Sure. I was called a tomboy, sometimes I still am. Most girls in fifth grade are never really basketball fans, so when your one of three playing with all the boys, you're pretty much an outcast until you become secure with yourself and proceed with what you love."

Janelle recalled watching the Phoenix Mercury versus the New York Liberty at Madison Square Garden in 2006. Even though she was in New York, she openly cheered for the Mercury because of Diana Taurasi. For Janelle it was the first time she saw women at that skill level play live basketball. "I was wowed. Becky Hammon was phenomenal with around twenty-five points. Diana Taurasi was amazing. The lay-ups, amazing crossovers, and—the one thing I love most—the three pointers were unbelievable. It was amazing," said Janelle.

After practice one evening, Janelle finally told me why she loved the game. She said, "Mostly the feeling—knowing—that I helped contribute with one basket, the control of holding the ball, the satisfaction of knowing hours of practice have paid off with a great jump shot, and the ability to be aggressive and be rewarded for it. I know I'll never play professional basketball, but that doesn't matter at all. I think it's important to watch women's sports live or on television because if I don't support, respect, and enjoy the women's game, I can't complain when men, or the majority of America don't support women's basketball."

My, How Things Have Changed

For Shay, Kristin, and Janelle, playing organized basketball is about the experience of it, the sheer enjoyment of being active.

Because let's not forget it wasn't too long ago that girls weren't given the opportunity to play organized sports at all.

When Donna Lopiano grew up, there was no Title IX, and there were no leagues for girls. "As is true of many women in my generation, the encouragement to play sports was a function of either growing up with a whole bunch of brothers or living on a street with a whole bunch of boys, where your parents didn't stop you from playing. Although I didn't have the brothers, I grew up on a street with fifteen boys and one other girl. Those kids always picked me first because I was a great athlete, and they didn't care whether I was a girl or not. So I'm sure that among all the sports that I played, these are the places of my fondest memories, having a hoop in the backyard, having an organized league on your street, two-on-two basketball, and playing everyday," said Lopiano.

Will Kristin ever make it to the WNBA? It doesn't really matter, does it? She and every other girl out there are at the very least provided the opportunity to try unlike the generations before. These young girls have role models now, female role models and professional basketball players to boot. They have a WNBA to aspire to. They have the Olympic Games to dream of. Too often we adults forget that sports are supposed to be fun. It's also about remembering what it feels like to play again—what it feels like to pursue one's own singular perfection—to live life rather than be lived by it. George Sheehan wrote in *Sport and Religion*, "Play is where life lives. Where the game is the game. At its borders, we slip into heresy. Become serious. Lose our sense of humor. Fail to see the incongruities of everything we hold to be important. Right and wrong become problematical. Money, power, position become ends. The game becomes winning. And we lose the good life and the good things play provides."[1]

At the youth participation level, it's important to recognize the freedom young girls now have to become acquainted with different sports and learn healthy habits in the process. The vast majority of young girls who play youth basketball will not grow up to play in the WNBA or the Olympic Games, and most of them are realistic enough to understand that, but at least they have the opportunity to dream.

Dawn Staley, former WNBA player who also has three Olympic gold medals to her name as a player and was the head coach of the Temple University women's basketball team, wrote a letter after her final game as a player. Dawn wrote, "I'm losing my first love. I think this is the love I will never get over. You know . . . 'The One.'"[2] If we allow our little girls to fall in love with the game, it may lead somewhere spectacular. Alternatively it may mean that they'll grow up and coach a youth basketball team.

On Your Mark, Get Set, Coach!

Coaching youth basketball is the most fun I've ever had on a basketball court. All this makes me wonder, Why don't more young women get involved in coaching? Why can't we stay involved after our playing days are complete?

Donna Lopiano suggests that there is no single cause why women aren't coaching. Lopiano suggests that women have not given up their primary-care responsibilities. Dad hasn't come to the rescue and said now you can coach. The female is still carrying the bulk of childcare and house care responsibilities in our society, and that goes for women who have the potential to be coaches too. Where there are single parent-households, the majority of parents are women. That keeps a large group of women out of the volunteer coaching role. "The fact that women are underpaid in general in our society takes women out of a lot of extracurricular activities, which if they didn't have to hold two jobs or work longer hours, would be available to them," said Lopiano.

Lopiano believes it's just a matter of timing. The first generation of women who played sports under Title IX is just beginning to coach. These women became old enough to coach in youth sports about five years ago. "We're also seeing the first generation of mom athletes coaching their children now. You don't see large numbers, because this is just the first wave—we haven't had time for it to be at critical mass," said Lopiano. Ten years from now, she believes it will be a very different picture.

Lopiano is quick to point out that when Title IX went into effect there wasn't instantly 900 percent more women participating in sport. It was a very gradual growth process. Similarly the number of women who were athletes and are now coaching their children is relatively small, but it will grow. "Essentially when you realize that the average woman doesn't have a child until she's thirty, we still have a ways to go," said Lopiano.

Progress may seem slow, but in reality the progress of the women's game has been extremely quick. In the thirty-five years Title IX has been in effect, record numbers of girls and young women began participating. Record numbers of women are entering fields of coaching and athletic administrative positions. Already four of the WNBA's thirteen head coaches are women. As women participate in intercollegiate sports and move onto other careers, the impact will most certainly be felt sooner rather than later. The key, however, is not to apply too much pressure to young girls when they first become acquainted with the sport.

The Role of Youth Sports

Drs. Ryan Hedstrom and Daniel Gould, from the Institute for the Study Youth Sports at Michigan State University, addressed the role of the youth-sports coach in *Research in Youth Sports*. They claim that the youth-sport coach can have a dramatic influence on young athletes' development and enjoyment of sport. They ask, "Who is the youth sport coach? The background and perspective of youth sport coaches can vary from inexperienced parent-volunteers to highly skilled and paid coaches of elite youth programs. Within this spectrum are millions of individuals that coach youth programs of all types."[3]

Dr. Gould said, "If I coach fourth- and fifth-grade girls' basketball, there is no doubt in my mind that my primary role is to make sure all those kids have a great time and fall in love with activity. Part of being successful at doing that is to make sure they have good fundamental skills." Crystal Robinson, assistant coach with the Washington Mystics and former WNBA player said, "It's important for female athletes to have good coaches who teach them the right things. I've seen so many talented players not make it because they were not taught the right way. That's the key."

Toni Messina is a sixth-grade teacher who has coached Catholic Youth Organization (CYO) girls' and boys' basketball in Westchester, New York, for over fifteen years. Messina has truly enjoyed watching the girls' athletic development over the years. "I began coaching this particular group of kids in third grade. They're now graduating high school and have played for their varsity team. Recently one of the players introduced me as her favorite coach. That meant so much to me."

Messina recalls first teaching the girls when they couldn't dribble, couldn't shoot, or even reach the basket. "To work with them for so many years and to see the progress they have made and how they have developed as a team, is probably one of the greatest things that I could take away from the experience," said Messina.

Messina also mentioned the additional pressure some parents tend to put on their kids, particularly at early ages. She said, "I've seen a lot of parents want their kids on a certain team. They want their kid on the A team because the parents assume there is some kind of stigma attached to playing on a lower level." In her experience, many parents don't see the big picture. They don't realize that it's really about their daughter learning the game. "It's about their daughter playing the game and being given the opportunity to improve her skills. If we place kids on a team where they are enjoying themselves, having fun, and improving, then we've done the right thing for that kid, regardless of whether it's an A or B team. Sometimes parents don't see that," said Messina.

Wendy Haft is currently the assistant athletic director at Rye Country Day School (RCDS) in Rye, New York. RCDS is a coeducational college preparatory school begun in 1869 dedicated to educating students from prekindergarten through grade twelve. Haft completed her BA at Ithaca College as a physical-education major and coached in the local community up in Ithaca. She then became a high-school coach and ran a junior hoops program for kids in fourth through sixth grades at Greenwich Academy. From there she went back to Ithaca to complete her master's degree in physical education with a minor in sports psychology. She was the assistant athletic director and head of physical education at King and Low-Heywood Thomas School, a private college preparatory school in Stamford, Connecticut, before coming to RCDS.

Haft started the Girls in Rye Love Sports program on weekends with some of the other coaches at RCDS. "A couple of coaches ran clinics for boys, but it seemed like there weren't many female role models interested in sports," said Haft. "We began a clinic for girls, and within a year had nearly thirty girls for an age group. Those numbers even surprised us. It showed a need, a need we filled."

Haft believes the biggest goal for the youth-sports coach is in understanding. She said, "Understanding that youth—and not just girls—require an enjoyable environment, the youth-sports coach must teach them how to be both competitive and skilled." Haft doesn't believe that girls who play sports are more or less competitive than their nonathlete peers, but parents tend to put them in more competitive situations. "I don't know if that's necessarily good; that added pressure is why girls tend to drop a sport so quickly."

In discussing the biggest challenges youth coaches face, Haft acknowledged that it's their schedules. She explained, "The biggest challenge in coaching kids is their busy schedules because it becomes less fun for the kids to be doing so much." Unfortunately, Haft doesn't believe there are enough truly qualified coaches. She said, "There are too many teams to always have qualified people coaching."

Haft also suggests that just because you know the game doesn't mean you'll make a good youth coach. "Your best coaches are great teachers, and just because you can teach doesn't mean you can coach. Plenty of coaches out there have no clue how to teach. They know the sport, and they love the sport. Maybe if they were coaching robots, that would be fine," said Haft.

Athletes who play in college participate because they want to play, but fun is not the primary goal. According to Haft, that philosophy has been handed down to the younger levels where too many coaches say, "If you don't like it, then leave." Haft wonders what the goal in that kind of environment really is, and it makes her question the philosophy of youth sports. Ultimately Haft believes that the philosophy in teaching youth sports should be twofold. First, sports should accommodate a wide spectrum of kids. Youth sports should do everything from encourage girls to improve, to want to improve, and to want to compete and understand that not everyone has the same role on a team. Second, Haft said, "It's about life lessons. Most of those kids are not necessarily going to play in high school or college. Youth sports are not for just the kids who will be playing high-school sports, so the youth coach must teach life lessons and team spirit and how to improve."

Doris Burke, basketball analyst said, "Well, I'll tell you this, as many strides as the women's game has taken, there is still a great need for quality individuals at the lower levels of basketball." People, both men *and* women who are passionate about the game must get involved at the lower levels. It's vital to the progression of the sport.

Mike McManus, former head women's basketball coach at St. Thomas Aquinas College in Sparkill, New York, wants parents to realize that the number-one reason why a child should play sports is for fun. Like Dr. Gould, McManus doesn't believe in sports specialization at too early an age because the option for fun is destroyed. He believes that thirteen years old is the magic age because then kids begin to understand what they really like and can better decide if they want to specialize in one particular sport.

Christina Wielgus, head coach of the Dartmouth College (New Hampshire) women's basketball team advises parents to allow their child to actually play and to allow children to learn the lessons of loss and disappointment in competition. Wielgus makes a distinction between disappointment and devastation. She said, "Not making a team is disappointing. Losing a sibling is devastating. Somehow that gets confused." If parents allow children to experience the ups and downs of competition on their own, in the long run they are empowering their children to manage themselves. Wielgus advises parents to help their kids get to where they're going safely and then step back and just let them play: "Parents should be thankful that their child has a passion because that passion will allow the child to grow. It will keep her out of trouble and get her through tough teen years. My goal as a parent is not for my sons to play in the NBA.

It's to get them busy enough and productive enough where they don't get into trouble."

WNBA superstar Diana Taurasi advises young girls not to worry about the future. She said, "Just concentrate on enjoying yourself, and really getting the most out of yourself, both in basketball and in life." Remember to enjoy the present more than anything else. That's advice we can all use in every walk of life. Because after all basketball is a sport. It's meant to be enjoyed.

Part two High-School Basketball

3 You Can't Measure Heart

As a high-school assistant coach, I'm constantly trying to find ways to communicate my love of the game with my players so that it rubs off on them. My primary goal in this endeavor is not to rack up more wins (although that's always nice) but to teach them a respect for the game that will hopefully carry over far beyond their playing days.

Last season during a particularly lackluster practice, I pulled the third string together and sat them down for a heart-to-heart talk. My problem wasn't their lack of skill, it was their lack of energy. "Whenever I step out onto a court, it is a blessing. Every moment I spend with a ball in my hands is a gift," I told them. I explained that while they might not see a minute of actual game time that season, it was their responsibility to their teammates and to themselves to put forth the best effort. Otherwise what lesson are they learning? Skim by unnoticed, and you'll go far?

My version of the ole "Give It All You Have Speech" is repeated thousands of times a season at all levels of the sport. Every now and then a player gets it. Every once in a while a coach gets the opportunity to work with a player who has competitive fire, skill, and work ethic. Those players and those moments shared are always memorable—not for the wins that probably accompany that player but for the sheer beauty in working with an athlete who genuinely loves the game of basketball.

Hayley O'Neil, a former cocaptain at Rye Country Day School was one of those players for me. As a senior O'Neil scored 317 total points, averaging 12.7 points per game. She had 112 total rebounds (4.5 per game) and 116 total assists (4.6 per game). She led her team to an unprecedented 20-6 record and to the New York State Association of Independent Schools class C championship game. O'Neil received the team's MVP award in 2007. She was named All-League FAA (Fairchester Athletic Association) for the second year in the row, All-League NEPSAC (New England Preparatory School Association) for the second year in a row, in addition to a host of tournament MVPs and all-tournament teams. O'Neil is one of the first players in the RCDS program history to play National Collegiate Athletic Association (NCAA) college basketball. She's at Connecticut College and will hopefully make an impact on their program.

O'Neil said, "I love the game because if you practice and work hard, you will see the results. It's easy to pick out those players who spend a great deal of time in the gym. Above all the feeling of scoring a basket outweighs any other good feeling in my day." O'Neil believes that there is a certain mentality needed to be a great basketball player. Like in any other sport, you must be willing to sacrifice yourself for the team—throw your body around, dive on the floor, be aggressive toward the opponent, and have your mind absolutely set that you will win. You obviously need to be in excellent physical shape—speed, athleticism, and height are all helpful.

I had the pleasure of coaching O'Neil at RCDS for two seasons.

She is without a doubt one of the hardest workers I have ever seen, let alone coached. Looking at her slender five-feet-eight-inch build off the court, you'd never imagine her power on the court. She isn't a vocal leader, choosing rather to lead by example. Her unselfishness and unbelievably strong work ethic made it a pleasure to coach her. The term "coach's dream" came up often when O'Neil was discussed. I wish every player was like her, but in truth they are not. Some players just don't work that hard, assuming their natural abilities will miraculously take them anywhere they wish to go. Others can't perform in big moments, but the good players, the really good ones, learn something vital in the losses.

Basketball players often learn more about themselves in the defeats than they do in the wins. Everyone wants to know a winner. Everyone wants to high-five a winner and relive her glory on the court. No one wants a quote from a loser. It's the winners' locker rooms that are full of reporters toting mini–tape recorders. "How did it feel," they all want to know. "How did you feel hitting the game-winning shot for your team," they all ask the winner in unison.

No one wants to ask a loser how it feels to lose because everyone knows that it hurts, and we tend to hide the hurt behind closed doors and shadowed eyes. The losses are harder to swallow, more difficult to overcome. Losses teach you how to cope with disappointment. Losses remind you that you have flaws and that some other players have fewer than you do. Losses show you that God, or whatever higher power you believe in, has granted superior physical abilities to someone else, but the trick played on athletes has nothing to do with talent because the heart of a champion often beats quietly inside a loser, just waiting for a chance to show itself.

You can't measure heart. There will never be a test that will effectively gauge it. Mediocre teams have beaten superior ones on heart alone. Human beings since the beginning of time have erupted from difficult circumstances to attain glorious achievements because of the desire in their hearts that only they knew was present all along, because talent only gets you so far.

Every winner was once a loser. Every winner once felt the

pain of being less than adequate. What separates the winners from the losers? Winners hate the taste of losing so much they'll do absolutely anything to avoid it, no matter how difficult or unpleasant the work of improving may be.

Life Lessons

Karen Eilbacher, a student at New York University and former high-school basketball player at RCDS, hates to lose at anything. Fiercely loyal to her love of the game even though she no longer plays basketball competitively, Eilbacher explained her first connection to the game this way: "I started playing basketball when I was in my mother's womb. I used her umbilical cord as both the ball *and* the hoop."

Eilbacher doesn't recall exactly when she gravitated toward the game. Having an athletic older sister definitely influenced her. "If I could keep up with my sister, it meant I could spend more time with her, which I loved," said Eilbacher. She doesn't really understand where her basketball talent came from, but for her everything on the court is natural, and she realized that at a very young age.

Stephanie Vaiano, a five-feet-seven-inch guard from Queens County, New York, played basketball at Archbishop Molloy High School in Briarwood, New York. Archbishop Molloy is a century-old academically competitive Catholic high school, which began admitting girls in 2000. For Vaiano basketball is not just a sport. She said, "It's more like the feeling I get when I step on the court. Every second, every minute, every hour, every day of practice, I must prove myself to my teammates, to my coaches, and to myself. I love the feeling I get when I'm driving hard to the basket, faking right, crossing over, faking left, and then laying the ball up in the basket."

Vaiano admitted that in order to be a good basketball player, you just have to do the work. She ticked off a list of sacrifices: three hours practices starting 8:00 a.m. on a Saturday while the rest of the world is sleeping, running suicides, lifting weights, staying after practice to work on a jump shot, spending time in the gym during the hot summer months. "In those moments, I push myself to run harder, to concentrate more. I want to make every lay-up, foul shot, and jump shot count. I want to get low on defense and keep my hands up at all times. There's absolutely nothing I don't love about this game: the coaches screaming, the tough practices, the intense games, and the teamwork. Every game and every practice I play in, I play like it's my last," said Vaiano. After twelve years of playing basketball, Vaiano couldn't imagine her life without basketball being a part of it. She credits basketball for teaching her discipline, dedication, and determination.

One of Vaiano's former teammates, a six-feet-one-inch post player named Angelina Waterman was also one of New York State's leading volleyball players in addition to being a solid basketball player. The Ozone Park native agreed with Vaiano that basketball is much more than just a hobby. Waterman explained, "Basketball is the way I live my life! There's a difference between someone who just plays basketball and someone who considers herself a basketball player. As a basketball player, there is nothing I love more than being on the court and having a basketball in my hands. Whether I'm working on post moves in practice or driving to the basket in the game, I always enjoy playing the sport I have dedicated myself to."

Waterman like so many other athletes and coaches believes that basketball has many similarities to life. Just as you take shots in the game, you take shots in life. Sometimes you win and sometimes you lose, but when it's all said and done, you know you have given everything you have and that you took your best shot.

Waterman remembers playing in an all-boys' basketball tournament when she was nine years old: "When the boys in the tournament realized they would play against me, a girl, they laughed and immediately assumed that I couldn't keep up with them. As soon as I stepped onto the court, I knew I had to prove myself as a basketball player." After the final buzzer sounded, she knew she had left an everlasting impression with those boys and everyone else watching that day. "All the compliments I received after the game from those who had doubted my abilities let me know that I accomplished something special," Waterman said.

Waterman's goal is to leave a lasting impression on anyone watching her play. She said, "I make it my job to give 110 percent during every practice, every game, and every scrimmage. I want to prove myself to everyone watching that I have great potential to become the best player I can become."

Nicole Boutte, originally from Carson, California, played for James Anderson at basketball powerhouse, Narbonne High School. Nicole said basketball taught her that attitude is everything and that she must always think positive. She said the game taught her to fight through anything and never give up. As if that's not enough of a life lesson, she also credits basketball for teaching her to never let the people who want her to fail bring her down. "Always stand tall and proud. Never hold back. Play like it's a championship game every moment of every day," said Boutte.

Boutte's former teammate from Narbonne, Janita Session, said, "I play because it gives me something to look forward to every day. I've learned that you must be able to communicate positively with people. You must be able to trust the people in your surroundings. You must be able to lead, not take total control of things in order to be successful. Believe in yourself and know that you can do anything you put your mind to. Last but not least, you must be able to share. Never be selfish because what you do unto others comes right back around to you."

Numbers Don't Lie

Had Title IX not been passed, these young women might never have learned the life lessons basketball teaches. They might never have experienced how to be a leader or how to work hard, vital lessons for any high-school student to learn.

According to a 2004–5 High School Athletics Participation Survey conducted by the National Federation of State High School Associations (based on competition at the high-school level in the 2004–5 school year) basketball was the most popular girls' program, with 456,543 participants.[1] According to the same study, in 1971–72 a mere 294,015 girls participated in sports. The following year that number jumped to 817,073. Title IX may not be the only factor contributing to such high numbers, but it certainly is a primary reason for such growth. A year later in 1973–74, over a million girls participated in sports (1,300,169). Exactly twenty years later, that number blossomed to 2,130,315.[2] According to a longitudinal study by Acosta and Carpenter in 1996, "participation opportunities for women athletes by the late 1990s hit an all-time high," so it's really no surprise that in 2004–5 girls' participation set an all-time record with a total of 2,908,390.[3]

Research conducted in 1991 by Skip Dane of Hardiness Research in Casper, Wyoming, revealed the following about participation in high-school sports: "The ratio for girls who participate in sports and do well in school is three to one. About 92 percent of sports participants do not use drugs. School athletes are more self-assured. Sports participants take average and above-average classes. Sports participants receive above-average grades and do above average on skills tests. Those involved in sports have knowledge of, and use financial aid, thus improving their chances to finish college. Student-athletes appear to have more parental involvement than other students. Students involved in athletics appear to change focus from cars and money to life accomplishments during the process."[4]

A 1989 nationwide study by the Women's Sport Foundation indicated that athletes do better in the classroom, are more involved in school activity programs, and stay involved in the community after graduation. The study also revealed that "high school athletic participation has a positive educational and social impact on many minority and female students." The study, based on an analysis of data collected by the U.S. Department of Education's High School and Beyond Study, indicated that "girls receive as many benefits from sports as boys. The 'dumb jock' stereotype is a myth. Sports involvement was significantly related to a lower dropout rate in some school settings. Minority athletes are more socially involved than non-athletes."[5]

A separate study done by the Center for the Social Organization of Schools at Johns Hopkins University found that sports had a "small but consistent" impact on a variety of other positive school outcomes too. The more involved that tenth graders were in athletics, for example, the more likely they were to feel confident of their academic abilities or to be engaged in their schools.[6]

The table in appendix A from the 2004–5 National Federation of High Schools High School Athletics Participation Survey clearly illustrates the high-school girls' participation in basketball broken down by state, with Michigan leading the way with over seventy thousand girls participating in basketball, followed by California at over thirty thousand.

All of this research means one thing: more high-school girls are becoming physically active, with basketball their number-one choice. However, all this interest and participation has its downsides too. With the WNBA firmly entrenched in the professional sports landscape and with increasing popularity in NCAA women's basketball, the competition and pressure for high-school basketball players to land college scholarships is creating an alarming trend.

Players like Becky Hammon and Ticha Penicheiro don't get to the WNBA on talent alone. They make it by working hard, performing well, and, perhaps most importantly, by being seen. The high-school recruiting process is not only present, but it is also highly competitive. High-school recruiting is considerably different than college recruiting. Private schools and Catholic schools can recruit heavily because those schools don't require that the student live in a certain district. Public schools can recruit, but it means that if the family doesn't live in a "basketball visible" district, they have to pick up and move their entire families in order for the student to play at a particular public school. It's not uncommon for families to make tremendous sacrifices so that their daughters can play for a specific coach or be in a specific school district known for basketball.

Dr. Dan Gould from the Institute for the Study of Youth Sports at Michigan State University believes that many parents are naive with respect to the high-school recruiting process. He gave an example to illustrate his point: Your daughter is a point guard in middle school. She wins a few games, and everyone congratulates you for having such a talented kid. Other parents and coaches tell you how talented your kid is, and they urge you to sign her up for summer camps and tournaments. Suddenly, everyone around you is talking about college scholarships. After a while other parents begin to ask you for advice since your kid is so successful. Suddenly, your abilities as a parent are reinforced by your daughter's success.

Dr. Gould believes that our culture reinforces two objectives: winning and rankings. The better your kid is at sports, the higher the reward potential (that is, college scholarships). The more parents invest financially and the more they invest emotionally, the more pressure there is for a return on that investment. "Parents get sucked into the return on the investment versus focusing on how great it is that their daughter feels better about herself," said Dr. Gould. He makes it clear that he is not opposed to athletic scholarships for boys or girls: "To me, a scholarship is icing on the cake. Personal and physical development should be first and foremost in the mind of a parent."

That personal and physical development includes nurturing the mind-set of a champion. We see champions in all walks of life—from single moms to dads who work two jobs to entrepreneurs, doctors, and teachers. The skills we learn in sports help us determine the way we will live our lives. Will we give up when things get tough? Will we put forth the extra effort? Will we stand back up when we get knocked down? The heart of a champion is strong. It's fierce, and it **never** gives up, whether on the court or off of it.

4 The Crème of the Crop

The key for young girls interested in the sport of basketball may very well be to have fun and enjoy the experience. However, once a talented athlete reaches high school, the game changes. Some have argued that the pressure placed on high-school athletes is far too intense, that fun has been removed from the equation. Players don't just work on basketball during the season anymore. They play twelve months a year. There is also a distinct difference between the program I coach in at Rye Country Day School and a program like Christ the King's. RCDS is absolutely more focused on academics. Students cannot practice more than an hour and a half per day. We cannot run practices on Sundays or during extended holiday breaks. For our program it's about being competitive within the framework we have been given. Not all schools operate on that level. This is not to suggest that powerhouse programs break any rules. There are, however, different levels of competitiveness within the high-school league structure.

The Christ the King High School Lady Royals are known across the country as being one of the elite high-school girls' basketball programs in the country. Coached by Bob Mackey, they have been Brooklyn-Queens Catholic High School Athletic Association League Champions for twenty-three consecutive years and have won seventeen consecutive Catholic State Championships. They were ranked the number-one high school-women's varsity basketball team in the country in 1990, 1993, 1998, 2005, and 2006 by *USA Today*. Seattle Storm point guard Sue Bird and recently retired Los Angeles Sparks guard Chamique Holdsclaw both attended Christ the King. From the 2002–3 varsity team, seven seniors signed with Division I programs, receiving full scholarships to those institutions. Among them Shay Doron (Maryland) would go on to play in the McDonalds All-American Game and then to play for the New York Liberty. Mackey topped one hundred wins in four years as head coach but more importantly, he saw a great group of players move on to the next level.

The following season marked further success for Mackey's program:

During the 2004–5 season, Christ the King returned to the finals of the Nike Tournament of Champions. Led by Duke signee Carrem Gay and underclassmen Tina Charles, Christ the King defeated Piedmont 44–42 in the finals. The Lady Royals finished the year a perfect 27-0 and New York State Federation Champions. *USA Today* selected them as the number-one team in the country, naming Mackey as the High School Coach of the Year. The Women's Basketball Coaches Association also chose Mackey as National Coach of the Year and selected him to coach the All-American game at the Women's Final Four.

Born in the Bronx, Bob Mackey grew up in Rockaway Beach. He played high school basketball at Xavier High School in Manhattan. After playing a year at Oneonta State University, he caught the coaching disease at Oneonta High School. Upon graduation, Bob accepted a position at Tolentine High School. He was the junior varsity and assistant varsity coach under John Sarandrea. In 1988, Tolentine captured the mythical *USA Today* National Championship behind the play of the late St. John's star Malik Sealy. In 1991, after the tragic closing of Tolentine High School, Mackey accepted a position at Christ the King High School. For the next nine years, he was Vincent Cannizzaro's assistant. State championships followed in each of the following years, with national championships in 1993 and 1998. The new millennium saw Mackey move into the head coach's seat at Christ the King, following a 25-5 season with a record eleventh consecutive state title.[1]

One afternoon in September, I visited Christ the King High School in order to spend some time with Mackey. Mackey had recently been named athletic director in addition to his responsibilities as dean of discipline and girls' basketball coach. Mackey apologized for his basement office steps away from the gymnasium through which so many stellar players have passed over the years. While he hadn't quite settled in, the walls and bookshelves were already covered with trophies, photos, and plaques from professional athletes who graduated from Christ the King High School, commemorating his team and his program's immense success.

Mackey sat behind a large oak desk, rocking in a squeaky metal chair. During our interview he rarely was able to complete a thought without being interrupted by an athlete or staff member looking for assistance. He's one of those coaches who downplays his program as if he was a small-time coach from the suburbs. When I asked Mackey about his coaching philosophy, I didn't get much except, "We run extremely intense practices, college-level practices, really."

Mackey has continued to build a program that every player and coach in the nation recognizes. A simple walk through the gym to the trophy cases turns into a twenty-minute conversation about some of the great players and great moments in Christ the King's history—a miniature hall of fame tour. As we walked down the length of the trophy cases, Mackey laughed and said,

"You know, we can't even fit it all in the trophy cases anymore. I have an entire closet filled with memorabilia I just can no longer keep out here." That's definitely a problem most coaches would dream of having. Make no mistake Mackey is a demanding high-school coach. He demands excellence from his players. He demands that they focus every moment of every practice.

Given that Mackey has experienced such an incredibly high level of success thus far in his career, I wanted to know what his most memorable moment was. Mackey hesitated only slightly. After handling a few phone calls and interruptions, he told me, "Sure, we've had our share of wins and big game moments, but I take more pride in seeing my players develop and sign that scholarship letter. Knowing that they have earned a scholarship to college, that their education is paid for, and their parents no longer need to worry, that's the real thrill for me." He continued, "It's not about being a great individual player at Christ the King. You look at my players and our stats, we rarely have a player who will go out there and drop twenty or thirty points. We really stress the team concept here. We're disciplined, and not many players here average over ten a game because it's not about the individual."

That's a tough lesson for some athletes to learn, particularly the talented scorers. Teaching a basketball player that it's not always about scoring your average, whatever that average might be, is a difficult task. The game comes together when five players on the court work together. Every player has a role to fulfill. Some are scorers, some are rebounders, but the good teams usually have better than good coaches reminding every player that there is no "I" in "team."

God, Family, School, Basketball

James Anderson, former head coach of Narbonne High School in California, developed it into a West Coast high-school basketball superpower. Anderson said, "I've won everything you can win in high school. Our players have gone on to play in the WNBA. We've had kids win championships at Tennessee and Connecticut. But it's always about taking the ninth grader and teaching them the game of basketball."

For Anderson teaching his players valuable life lessons is more important than any trophy they might hoist over their heads. Over the past few years Anderson's teams have faced off against Mackey's teams several times. Anderson recalled, "The first time we met was the first year he took over at Christ the King, and we beat him. Our kids were jawing the whole game, it was just so intense."

Since undertaking his first basketball coaching assignment in 1992–93 at Narbonne High School, Anderson built a program that posted a combined 303-72 record over the past decade, which includes three California Interscholastic Federation (CIF) championships (1998, 2000, and 2001), adding the school's name to the elite roster of girls' high-school basketball programs nationwide. Even more impressive is his 89-7 record (.927 winning percentage) over his last three seasons as head coach at Narbonne. Anderson stepped down as head coach at Narbonne High School on October 31, 2006, citing administrative conflicts. He is currently the director of the OGDL (Olympians Girls Development League) Girls' Basketball Club Team and a member of the Women's Basketball Coaches Association (WBCA) High School All-American Game Selection Committee.

Anderson points to the regional semifinal game against Boyena High School in 1997 as having put his program on the map. "Boyena was a powerhouse. They had never lost in their gym and were picked to win states that year. We went to their gym and beat them. Boyena thought because we were an inner-city school that we could only play an up-tempo game, but that's not how we played. We ran our offense. We went on to lose in the regional final, but in that game, I knew we had something special."

Anderson received National Coach of the Year accolades from *USA Today* and from the National Federation of State High School Associations (NFHS) in 2000 and 2001. Additionally he earned a pair of CIF Coach of the Year awards in 1998 and 2000. His first CIF honor came in 1998 after finishing ranked number six in the country by *USA Today*, recording a 29-4 record and claiming Narbonne's first Division I state title. Two years later he received national honors from both *USA Today* and the NFHS, as well as his second CIF Coach of the Year nod after reclaiming the state championship with a perfect 34-0 record and catapulting his squad to the number-one position in the country as listed by *USA Today*. The following season, Anderson's squad again finished at the top of *USA Today*'s rankings again, posted a 28-3 record and claimed a second consecutive state title. For his efforts he not only attained his second *USA Today* Coach of the Year honor, but Anderson was also named the 2001 NFHS Coach of the Year. Most recently, Anderson's 2001-2 Narbonne team advanced to the CIF regional finals, went 27-4, and was ranked fourteenth in the country by *USA Today*.

No fewer than fifteen of Anderson's players have gone on to compete in the NCAA, including 2001 USA Basketball Junior World Championship Team bronze medalist, Loree Moore (Tennessee, New York Liberty); as well as USC's standout and 2000 USA Basketball Junior World Championship Qualifying Team gold medalist, Ebony Hoffman (USC, Indiana Fever); Connecticut's Willnet Crocket; and University of Southern California's Jessica Cheeks and Portia Mitchell.

Anderson never expected to coach. In 1983-84 his father created the Olympians Girls Development League thanks to a grant from the Olympic Committee, and Anderson helped any way he could. Lisa Leslie (Los Angeles Sparks) and Tina Thompson (Houston Comets) played in that league, just to name two.

Anderson believes that over the years, he's mellowed considerably. "I've coached boys and girls. I know some people coach boys differently than girls. I coach the same way. I scream, I do all the same things. Basketball is basketball. Successful coaches at all levels just teach the game," said Anderson.

Anderson is another coach who has noticed the pressure parents place on their daughters. "There is a fantasy that players can make millions of dollars like they do in the NBA." He believes that too many players and their parents think there's a pot of gold at the end of the rainbow in girls' basketball. He said, "We're in the MTV era where kids want it now, parents want it now. They want more." He's told his players more than once, "If we had your parents' intensity, we'd never lose a game." He said that too many parents are living through their kids: "As long as a kid is working hard and trying to give herself a fair chance, then that's all anyone can ask. Too often, they act like it's a birthright."

Anderson has always been realistic. For him, it's about God, family, school, basketball, and then friends. "We try to keep the kids rooted in discipline. We teach our kids to use the game to get a great college degree, if they can — play basketball in college if they are able to, [and] if they're not, at least to use the discipline and teamwork they learned to help themselves in life."

The Elephant in the Room: AAU

The Amateur Athletic Union (AAU) is the largest nonprofit, multisport, volunteer service organization in the United States. It's dedicated to the promotion and development of amateur athletes and to promote good sportsmanship and good citizenship. The unwritten rule in high-school basketball is this: If you're good or serious about hoops, you had better become involved in AAU.

According to the AAU's publicity materials:

The AAU was founded in 1888 to establish standards and uniformity in amateur sport. During its early years, the AAU served as a leader in international sport representing the U.S. in the international sports federations. The AAU worked closely with the Olympic movement to prepare athletes for the Olympic games. After the Amateur Sports Act of 1978, the AAU has focused its efforts into providing sports programs for all participants of all ages beginning at the grass roots level. Over 500,000 participants and over 50,000 volunteers share the philosophy of "Sports for All, Forever." The AAU is divided into 57 distinct districts. These districts annually sanction more than 34 sports programs, 250 national championships and over 30,000 age division events.

The AAU basketball program was established in 1972 as part of the AAU Junior Olympic program. Prior to 1972, the AAU Men's and Women's Committee conducted basketball championships, which included a single junior division. The national championships started in two age divisions

(15/under and 18/under) and have expanded to nine (10/under-18/under) plus the Junior Olympic Games, the National Invitational Championships (NICS), and the 10–13 Western Championship. In 2003, 751 teams competed for 10 AAU Girls' Basketball National Championship crowns, with 288 additional teams playing in our D-II National Championships.[2]

Virtually every coach and player at all levels mentioned AAU when I talked to them. Players overwhelmingly point out its necessity, particularly with regard to getting recruited. Coaches, on the other hand, seemed to believe the AAU has caused some problems with regard to players' and parents' attitudes.

My personal experience with AAU wasn't terribly positive. I had no interest in becoming part of the "recruiting mechanism." As much as I loved basketball, AAU seemed disjointed for me—like everyone was out for herself. I played AAU for two summers then gave it up. It just never felt comfortable for me.

Mike McManus, former head women's coach for St. Thomas Aquinas College, a Division II program, believes AAU has gotten out of control and is no longer a positive experience for the elite athletes. As he recruits players for his program, he's noticed that the high-school coach has been forgotten in a lot of respects: "I deal more with AAU coaches than high-school coaches in some cases and that gives some people more power than they really should have."

According to McManus, it's all about scholarship dollars. He and many other coaches believe that many AAU teams are created because a parent is unhappy with their kid's playing time at the high-school varsity level. "There are so many parents who don't understand what competition is all about. They don't understand the hard work to become a starter or to play is a necessary part of the process," said McManus.

Patrick McKee, member of the AAU Girls Basketball National Committee, said, "Many of the teams that participate in AAU girls' basketball programming do so for all the right reasons and have a terrific experience. Many coaches are directing teams properly and with care. Some coaches, however, aren't as qualified as they should be or have agendas beyond merely coaching teams." McKee believes that the same is true in college basketball and high-school basketball: "The coaches who are not good generally don't last in those positions, and all of college basketball and all of high-school basketball is not labeled as 'out of control' because of those coaches who are not good ones."

Eddie Clinton, senior sports manager of AAU Sports, stated that AAU participation numbers have leveled off over the last few years, primarily because of the proliferation of other organizations offering opportunities. According to Clinton, that is both a blessing and a curse. "The blessing is that it gives more girls an opportunity to play, particularly at the local level. However, to us that has become somewhat of a curse. It used to be that all summer basketball was AAU. That is no longer the case, but many people, including high-school and even college coaches, still believe that to be the case."

Christina Wielgus, head women's basketball coach at Dartmouth College, isn't the only coach who sees problems with AAU. She said, "I don't like AAU, but if parents want their children to be recruited, they have to go through AAU."

According Patrick McKee, many college and high-school coaches confuse the official AAU basketball program with any nonschool spring and summer event. The official AAU events in most cases are pretty well organized with a rulebook, policies, and a democratic organizing body. Beyond that, official AAU events have been sanctioned from a district (state) or national office, and there is a mechanism to deal with issues that arise.

By contrast, many of the nonschool, spring and summer events for travel or club teams are not part of anything, certainly not officially part of the AAU. Their primary purpose is to generate funds for the event organizer, who often doesn't care very much about the event's quality once the entry fee has been collected. The name AAU being confused with the generic nonschool events is a problem, according to McKee.

Dianne Nolan, former head women's coach at Fairfield University and now assistant coach at Yale University, believes that frequency of games (sometimes three games a day) coupled with the pay to play mentality, creates a lack of competitiveness in athletes. That mentality doesn't serve the athletes well when they get to a different environment where it's all competition and only the best players play. "Right now, too many kids think if I just work hard, then I should play, but that isn't the case," said Nolan. "I'm not sure the entitlement is caused by AAU. AAU is the vehicle; parents apply too much pressure but AAU isn't the sole cause."

Jody Conradt, former head coach at the University of Texas and second winningest coach in NCAA history, said, "I believe that when you lose, it should be devastating. It should hurt. You should want to cry. With the way things are structured, it doesn't matter if you lose because you'll be playing again in twenty minutes."

Eddie Clinton from AAU believes that some of what Coach Nolan and Conradt said can also be attributed to the above-mentioned proliferation: "We don't allow more than two games a day except in a few circumstances. AAU is different than other endeavors. We have some great people and great coaches involved for all the right reasons. We also have some that don't have the same priorities." Further, Clinton believes the same thing can be said for girls' high-school coaches. Some coaches take pride in what they do and it shows in the quality of teams and individuals they produce. Unfortunately there are others who are just in that position because somebody is needed to show up. "Our motto here at AAU is 'Sports for All, Forever'; we want to offer unique opportunities to as many young ladies as possible and also allow those elite players a program [in which] to develop from elementary school to the WNBA and beyond," concluded Clinton.

The difficulty for the AAU is in finding the right balance of active participation for the less-intense athlete, and for the elite players.

Part three College Basketball

5 Three Divisions, One Association

From the moment I stepped onto the practice court at Mount Saint Mary College in Newburgh, New York, in October of 1991, I knew I had something to prove. I was on a self-imposed mission. Deep down next to all those things I held personal and sacred, I held pride. I wanted to prove to myself that I was a player, pure and simple. Although I never played in front of huge crowds and although I never played in a program that garnered television coverage or color commentary, I played nonetheless, and that experience shaped the kind of person I was to become.

I attended every practice my freshman season with the mind-set of a fighter training for a prizefight. I wasn't blessed with foot speed or jumping ability, but I was blessed with heart. I came in first or second in every sprint. I fought for every rebound and loose ball and never let up in practice. Frequently I came to practice early to work on my shooting and often stayed late.

My freshman year I scored over five hundred points, just four points shy of what I had scored in four years of high school. I scored a career-high and school record thirty-eight points in a single game. I led every statistical category except turnovers and blocked shots. I started every game and averaged over thirty minutes per contest. I won awards. I made dean's list. I joined campus groups and made certain my life did not entirely revolve around basketball. I was popular on campus and knew I had made the right choice in coming to Mount Saint Mary College.

I was proud of my accomplishments, but when people heard the name Mount Saint Mary College, a blank look usually ensued. More often than not, I was asked if I played for St. Mary's in Maryland. They made it to the Big Dance once or twice. People know the Big Dance. No one knows Division III. In the elite basketball circles, Division I is the place to be and to be seen. UConn, Tennessee, Duke, Notre Dame, LSU—these are the linchpins to Division I women's college basketball. Everyone knows about the NCAA tournament, and the UConn-Tennessee rivalry. On March 29, 2002, UConn defeated the Lady Vols in front of the largest crowd (29,619) in women's history, and it was the highest-rated basketball game, men's or women's, in television. The field of sixty-four never includes teams like Mount Saint Mary College. None of the players in Division III earn full scholarships to play basketball. Only Divisions I and II offer that, and the Ivy League in Division I is the exception because they do not allow athletic scholarships either.

Most athletes or parents never really understand how the NCAA is structured, but it is important to understand when looking at the breadth and scope of the organization, particularly with reference to how it relates to Title IX and opportunities for girls in sports.

According to the National Collegiate Athletic Association, the organization's core purpose is to "govern competition in a fair, safe, equitable and sportsmanlike manner, and to integrate intercollegiate athletics into higher education so that the educational experience of the student-athlete is paramount."[1]

According to the NCAA's background materials, the NCAA consists first of members. These members are the colleges, universities, and conferences that make up the NCAA. The national office, located in Indianapolis, Indiana, houses nearly four hundred paid staff members who implement the rules and programs established by the membership. The association is composed of members and staff. Many believe the association rules college athletics; however, it is actually a bottom-up organization in which the members rule the association.

Next the NCAA is broken down into three divisions. There are clear and distinct differences among each division. In order to be considered an NCAA program, a college or university must fit specified criteria:

Division I

Division I member institutions must sponsor at least seven sports for men and seven for women (or six for men and eight for women) with two team sports for each gender. Each playing season has to be represented by each gender as well. There are contest and participant minimums for each sport, as well as scheduling criteria. For sports other than football and basketball, Division I schools must play 100 percent of the minimum number of contests against Division I opponents—anything over the minimum number of games has to be 50 percent Division I. Men's and women's basketball teams have to play all but two games against Division I teams; for men, they must play one-third of all their contests in the home arena. Division I schools must meet minimum financial aid awards for their athletics program, and there are maximum financial aid awards for each sport that a Division I school cannot exceed.

Division II

Division II institutions have to sponsor at least five sports for men and five for women, (or four for men and six for women), with two team sports for each gender, and each playing season represented by each gender. There are contest and participant minimums for each sport, as well as scheduling criteria. Specifically with regard to women's basketball, teams must play at least 50 percent of their games against Division II opponents. There are not attendance arena game requirements for basketball. There are maximum financial aid awards for each sport that a Division II school must not exceed. Division II teams usually feature a number of local or in-state student-athletes. Many Division II student-athletes pay for school through a combination of scholarship money, grants, student loans and employment earnings. Division II athletics programs are financed in the institution's budget like other academic departments on campus.

Division III

Division III institutions have to sponsor at least five sports for men and five for women, with two team sports for each gender, and each playing season represented by each gender. There are minimum contest and participant minimums for each sport. Division III athletics features student-athletes who receive no financial aid related to their athletic ability and athletic departments are staffed and funded like any other department in the university. Division III athletics departments place special importance on the impact of athletics on the participants rather than on the spectators. The student-athlete's experience is of paramount concern. Division III athletics encourages participation by maximizing the number and variety of athletics opportunities available to students, placing primary emphasis on regional in-season and conference competition.[2]

The NCAA wasn't always so equitable with regard to women's sports. "The NCAA began administering women's athletics programs in 1980 when Divisions II and III established 10 championships for 1981–82. A year later, the historic 75th Convention adopted an extensive governance plan to include women's athletics programs, services and representation. The delegates expanded the women's championships program with the addition of 19 events."[3]

According to the *1981–82–2004–05 NCAA Sports Sponsorship and*

Participation Rates Report, "The number of NCAA championship sport teams in 2004–05 exceeded the previous all-time high from 2003–04, with increases coming from both men's and women's sports. The number of teams sponsored for women increased by 43 while the number sponsored for men increased only slightly by seven teams."[4]

In the same report, in 2004–5 52.9 percent of the championship sport teams in the NCAA were women's teams. The proportion of men's to women's teams is similar when looking at each division separately. As is the case with women's sports, there have been more men's basketball teams sponsored than any other men's sport, and in 2004–5 that trend continued.

Additionally, participation levels in NCAA sports were at an all-time high in 2004–5 for both male and female student athletes. There are now nearly 385,000 student athletes participating in sports for which the NCAA conducts championships. There are still more male student athletes (57.1 percent of the total) than female student athletes participating in championship sports. The proportion of male to female student athletes participating in NCAA championship sports is similar when looking at each division separately.[5]

Table 1 illustrates the difference in both teams and number of NCAA female athletes over the course of twenty-four years, beginning in 1981–82. Increased female athletic participation is evident at all levels of sport, including high schools, colleges, and universities.[6]

OK, so all this data boils down to one thing: more women are playing sports. More women are playing basketball. What does that mean? It means more people are watching women's sports on television, or want to watch more. It means women's basketball is slowly working its way into the mainstream consciousness. In addition as most things in life, that boils down to advertising dollars and cents.

Donna Lopiano believes the one bright light in terms of television coverage was the almost accidental occurrence of extensive coverage of collegiate women's basketball because of the nature of second-tier conference television contracts. While the process is complicated, the result was better exposure to

Table 1.	DIVISION I		DIVISION II	
	Teams	Athletes	Teams	Athletes
1981–1982	273	3,659	176	2,500
1991–1992	288	3,842	216	2,979
2001–2002	321	4,743	284	3,944
2004–2005	323	4,747	278	3,874

Source: NCAA, 1981–82–2004–05 NCAA *Sports Sponsorship and Participation Rates Report*

women's sports. Lopiano said, "In Division I, there was as real effort on the part of athletic directors to protect overexposure of their most valuable products, men's football and basketball. As a result, when they developed Ray-Com or Jefferson Pilot or other third-party conference contracts, which typically cherry pick games not aired as part of a national network or national cable telecast, schools insisted that in order to gain access to basketball or football, there had to be a required airing of at least X-number of women's sports and men's minor sports." Although the athletic directors did this in order to protect the value of their main properties, an accident in history resulted in a tremendous inventory of and a tremendous exposure for women's basketball on regional sports cable to the tune of two to three hundred games a season—big numbers. So these games on television became the advertising and promotional mechanism that grew the game and the audience for collegiate women's basketball.

Kristin Bernert, senior director, team business development at the WNBA, believes the connection to the schools and the alumni bases is also a driving force for increased exposure. The networks' commitment to the partnership with the NCAA has resulted in better exposure. "If people know that the games are on, they're going to watch them. I think that they've built a nice partnership with the NCAA and it's proven to be successful. It's benefited college women's basketball," said Bernert.

Bernert also believes that in turn collegiate women's basketball has benefited from the success of the WNBA. The chatter surrounding the WNBA draft picks helps; the increased exposure

DIVISION III		OVERALL	
Teams	Athletes	Teams	Athletes
256	3,465	705	9,624
306	4,058	810	10,879
412	5,837	1,017	14,524
424	6,065	1,025	14,686

(Indianapolis IN: NCAA, 2005).

of the WNBA helps collegiate exposure as well. "There is a mutual benefit between the NCAA and the WNBA in growing the game. Increased exposure in the NCAA and college women's basketball, the better it is for the WNBA, and vice versa. We both benefit from each other's success," Bernert said.

The benefits of success in increased exposure don't only revolve around ticket sales or fans filling the seats of large stadiums. It means that more girls will grow into women who have basketball as part of their core. That in turn means they'll grow up to become coaches, athletic administrators, or consumers of products by and about women's athletics.

Dianne Nolan became a career coach in a generation that has seen few women take on that challenge. In an even more unusual twist, she didn't need to look far for a role model in such a career. Nolan's mother coached girls' basketball at Gloucester Catholic. Her brother played college ball at Temple University. However, Nolan originally expected her career to be in athletic training. She was the first female athletic trainer at West Virginia University. "I covered the women's basketball team, and I absolutely hated sitting on the other end of the bench. I realized then that I really wanted to coach," said Nolan. Being around young people, the game, and the competition was a perfect fit for Nolan and unlike any other profession that she had considered. "I love the competitiveness of the game, the camaraderie of it. I like it because not very many people can do it. The game is just different every day. The challenges are different every day," expressed Nolan.

Nolan spent twenty-eight seasons at the helm of the Division

I, Fairfield University women's basketball program, with thirty-three years of coaching under her belt overall. Her combined career record is 517-416. She is now the assistant coach at Yale University.

On January 29, 2006, Nolan reached uncommon ground, becoming just the 28th coach in Division I women's basketball history to record 500 career wins. Her 517 career wins, ranked her 27th in career wins in NCAA Division I.

Nolan took over the Fairfield program in 1979, its second to last year at the Division II level. She oversaw the Stags' move to the Division I ranks for the 1981–82 season and then the move into the Metro Atlantic Athletic Conference (MAAC). Nolan came to Fairfield after five seasons as the head women's basketball coach at St. Francis College, in Brooklyn, New York, from 1974–79.[7]

Nolan's philosophy probably hasn't changed over the years, but her style has. She became a head coach at an incredibly young age (twenty-three years old). "I really was a bit of a pit bull because I wanted to make sure I was respected. Then as I matured, I found that my approach mellowed. I explained rather than demanded things," said Nolan. She believes that a coach's style needs to change as the players change: "Upbringings have changed, and the climate of the world has changed; a good coach must find a way to reach her student athletes."

Over the course of her career, Nolan has found ways to reach hundreds of student athletes.

Her 28-year tenure at Fairfield was the fifth longest among active coaches at one school, and was the ninth longest tenure in NCAA Division I women's basketball history. Her Fairfield tenure has been one to write home about, with four NCAA Tournament berths, a trip to the 2000 WNIT [Women's National Invitation Tournament], three MAAC Tournament Titles and three MAAC Regular Season crowns. Nolan led the Stags to their first-ever at-large bid to the NCAA Tournament in 2001.

The first conference title for Nolan came in 1988. Nolan led the Stags back to the NCAA Tournament in 1991, and for a third time as MAAC Champions in 1998. In 2001, Nolan and her team received their first at-large bid to the NCAA Tournament.[8]

Nolan recalled, "I remember when we were in the locker room on Selection Sunday. Wisconsin got in first. I looked over at the team and thought, *We're not in*, but the next announcement was Fairfield University. I jumped so high. It was pure elation. It felt like the good guys finally won."

Her dedication to promoting the sport of women's basketball is evident outside her coaching duties. She is in the midst of a three-year term as treasurer of the Women's Basketball Coaches Association (WBCA), the latest position in a long history of service to that organization, dating to 1981. In September 2006 she was named to the committee that selects the State Farm Wade Trophy winner, given annually by the WBCA to the Division I women's basketball player of the year.

Perhaps more important than the on-court success is the success Nolan-coached student athletes have had in the other avenues of their collegiate careers. Nolan stresses academics to her players, and every senior that she has coached at Fairfield has graduated with a degree on time—no small feat considering the university's high academic standards. Under Nolan Fairfield's women's basketball program boasted a 100 percent graduation rate. "Time management, fair play, and cooperation are all vital lessons student athletes take far beyond the lines of the court," said Nolan.

The lessons Nolan teaches her players have also served her well. "Personal accolades have also found their way to Nolan's office desk and walls. This past spring she was the recipient of the 2006 Metropolitan Basketball Writers Association Distinguished Service Award. Her coaching peers have voted Nolan the MAAC Coach of the Year five times during her illustrious career, in 1983, '84, '90, '98, and 2000. In 2001 she was named the MBWAA [Metropolitan Basketball Writers' Association] Coach of the Year and in 1984 was honored as the New England Coach of the Year."[9]

One of Nolan's former players appreciates Nolan's expertise and hard work. Clare Faurote graduated from Fairfield University in May of 2006. She was a cocaptain and four-year player for Nolan. In 2006 Faurote worked for Nolan as a graduate assistant while taking courses for her MBA in international business. Faurote said of Nolan, "I learned so much from Coach Nolan. As a player, you don't really realize how much a coach does. You take for granted how everything just falls into place. Now I realize how much there is to do, because I'm the one who has to help do it!"

Cara Murphy from Haddon Township, New Jersey, also played for Nolan. Murphy described her experience playing for Coach Nolan as tremendous. She said, "Coach Nolan is a great role model and lady. There is a buzz around her. Everyone knows her. The best part about her is how she has affected this community. Don't get me wrong she's a tough lady. She doesn't take bullshit at all. None. She was the first woman coach I had and has taught me so much. I'm so grateful for that."

Murphy's former teammate, Shirrell Moore from Mount Vernon, New York, has a special connection to her former coach. Nolan not only coached Moore but also coached her mother, Patrice Wallace, in 1979, Nolan's first season as head coach at Fairfield.

In a business where players come and go, Nolan remembers every one of her former players. "When I look at my wall of team photos, I know where all of those ladies are, and that probably means the most to me as a coach," said Nolan.

Like her mother, Moore absolutely loves the intensity, the enthusiasm, and the pace of the game. "I hate losing; I get that from my dad. After a loss I'm usually pretty upset. I usually don't talk at all and might even cry. If I do my best, then maybe I wouldn't be so angry about it, but if I lose and I know we could have won the game, then I can't talk to anybody without being angry," said Moore.

Nolan agrees, losing isn't fun at all, but to her doing the work to improve is. She also recognizes how important it is for women to see other women in leadership roles. Several of her former players have gone onto successful coaching careers. Nolan admits that if it weren't for her mother, she might never have caught the coaching bug.

6 Conradt, Goestenkors, and the Pursuit of Perfection

Few individuals in the sport of basketball, men's or women's, are synonymous with greatness. Multi-Hall of Fame legend and six-time National Coach of the Year, Jody Conradt is one of those individuals. The number of women she has inspired is incalculable.

Conradt resigned as head coach of the Division I University of Texas (UT) Lady Longhorns in 2007 after thirty-one memorable seasons (thirty-eight seasons coached overall). She built the UT program from the ground up, turning it into a powerhouse in the women's game. "When I started out, nobody cared whether we won or not. It wasn't on anyone's radar," said Conradt.

Today the University of Texas basketball program is very much on the radar, thanks in large part to the storied success Conradt enjoyed while at the helm. Her overall record after thirty-eight seasons in coaching and 1,207 games on the sidelines is 900-307 for a winning percentage of .746. At Texas her thirty-one-year record stands at 783-245 (.768 winning percentage) after 1,028 games on the Longhorns' sidelines (a .761 winning percentage). Her successor at Texas, Gail Goestenkors, said of Conradt, "She has been such a pioneer for women's basketball and a great ambassador for the game. She's been a great role model and a shining example for our sport."

With her coaching accomplishments elevating her to one of the best of all time, Conradt stands number-two in all-time career college basketball victories among all men's and women's coaches (active and nonactive). Her Texas teams reached the NCAA Final Four three times (1986, 1987, and 2003) with her 1986 squad capturing the NCAA championship with a perfect 34-0 mark—the first women's team in Division I history to go undefeated.

Conradt believes that the game of basketball creates a laboratory to develop lifelong skills, namely: focus, intensity, and a commitment to be diligent in pursuit of excellence. "Someone once said that basketball is five people on the floor sharing one basketball. I think that illustrates what you have to do as part of a team," said Conradt.

Speaking of life lessons, Conradt talked about her 1986 undefeated national championship team, but she also talked about the 1985 team that preceded it. In 1985 the University of Texas was scheduled to hold the Women's Final Four. "Tickets had been sold, we were ranked and seeded number one. It was all set for us to enjoy a really special moment," recalled Conradt. However, basketball has a way of surprising even the best prepared. With a buzzer-beating shot, Western Kentucky eliminated Coach Conradt and her Lady Longhorns by a score of 92–90. "Nothing was more devastating to know that we disappointed thousands of fans who had already bought tickets. We watched someone else win on our home floor. We watched someone else cut down the nets on our court," said Conradt.

The following preseason, Conradt noted a totally different motivation level on the part of her players and coaching staff. There was no discussion about who would become the star or who would receive the individual awards. "It was all total and complete unified focus to get past that horrible feeling from the year before, and as a result they went 34-0. We might have won because we were talented, but I have my doubts about whether or not they would have gone undefeated had it not been for living through the failure and adversity of the previous season," said Conradt.

Basketball is the pursuit of perfection, and generally we are not perfect at anything we do, especially in sports. Conradt admits that winning is a huge motivator, but within every athlete there is that fear of failure. "None of us likes to fail. None of us likes to look bad. None of us likes to be labeled losers. In basketball, it's on the scoreboard for everyone to see," said Conradt.

During Conradt's illustrious career, the scoreboard was usually lit up in her favor.

Conradt has been the recipient of numerous Hall of Fame and national coach of the year honors. In 1998–99, Conradt was enshrined into both the Naismith Memorial Basketball Hall of Fame in Springfield, Mass, becoming just the second women's basketball coach in history (following basketball coaching pioneer Margaret Wade) to be elected into the elite Hall. In 1995, the International Women's Sports Hall of Fame (New York City, 1995) enshrined her, where she joined her rightful place among such legendary sports pioneers as Babe Didrikson Zaharias, Betsy Rawls, Billie Jean King and Wilma Rudolph. Conradt also was a member of the inaugural class of inductees (26 inductees) into the 1999 Women's Basketball Hall of Fame in Knoxville, Tenn. In June 2003, she was inducted into the prestigious International Scholar-Athlete Hall of Fame (at the Institute for International Sport in Providence RI) in the summer of 2003.

She has been inducted into the Texas Women's Hall of Fame (1986), Texas Sports Hall of Fame (1998) and the UT Women's Athletics Hall of Honor (in the inaugural class of 2000). Conradt received the Carol Eckman Award in 1987, the highest honor given annually by the Women's Basketball Coaches Association (WBCA). In 1991, the National Association for Girls and Women in Sports awarded her for outstanding commitment to women's athletics. Conradt also received an award for her contribution to the sport from the NCAA during the 10th anniversary of the basketball championship in 1992. Conradt was one of seven finalists for Naismith Women's Basketball Coach of the Century honors.[1]

While many followers of the women's game assume that the athletes in the women's game today have become stronger, faster, and more athletic, Conradt differs with that opinion. She believes that there have always been extremely talented female basketball players. "Now, more talented players and more teams are playing at a higher level," she said. Rather than drawing attention to how the athletes may or may not have changed, Conradt suggested everything that happens within the boundaries of the court has stayed the same: "The same number of athletes on the court still plays by the same rules. The goal is the same height. I don't think anything has changed with regard to teaching the game, how much players want to be successful, or the lessons they learn by playing the game. However, everything outside of the boundaries of the court has changed."

Conradt sees our instant-gratification society trickle down to athletes who seek instant gratification in sports by winning, even though there are clear consequences for not doing the right thing: you foul five times, you're out. Poor decisions or lack of performance are evident every day in sports. "That becomes critically important in today's society because I don't see young people receiving consequences for negative behavior as much as they might have years ago," said Conradt. She also believes the women's game is at a crossroads. "I think our model is the men, no question. It would help if we could look at what has happened on the men's side and make better decisions, but we can't figure out how to be different and still be equal."

Conradt has serious concerns about the recruiting process and the system student athletes are subjected to. They must play twelve months a year just to keep up. "It's not healthy for the individual, and it's not healthy for our sport," said Conradt. Burnout is a difficult to substantiate with research, but Conradt urges a strong look at the increase in injuries on the women's side. She points to the trend with the professional athletes as cause for concern: "Even at the WNBA level, athletes play all year internationally and then jump into the WNBA. Think about the players who are injured on a regular basis. There is no time for recovery. It's bad for our game because we are creating an unreal environment for an athlete to succeed and stay healthy to the benefit to athletes or our sport."

Conradt's ties to the game of basketball go back a long way, and her pursuit of helping the women's game progress is unquestioned. "Conradt began her illustrious basketball career in Goldthwaite, Texas—a small town about 100 miles northwest of Austin. She was a prep standout in her own right, averaging 40 points per game for the GHS Eagles. [This was before the three-point shot was in existence.] Upon graduation from high school, Conradt headed to Waco, Texas, where she attended Baylor University, earning a degree in physical education in 1963 while averaging 20.0 points per game during her basketball career."[2]

Her interest in coaching was an accident. "I didn't go to college with the intent of coaching. At that time not many women had the intent of becoming doctors or lawyers either. Barriers had to be broken for us to change our dreams and expectations," recalled Conradt. She originally entered Baylor University with a dream of teaching. "I lived in a small town where the only professional women I saw were teachers, so I thought that's what I wanted to do," she said.

As she took classes for a degree in education, Conradt missed playing basketball and wanted to play. At Baylor she heard of a women's team that traveled on weekends at their own expense to compete against other colleges. The only way Conradt could join the team was to change her major to physical education. "I didn't really want to change majors, but my desire to be on a team and play basketball was so strong that I decided to give it a try," she explained. The contacts she made led her to her first coaching assignment. In the fall of 1969 Conradt made her entrance into the collegiate coaching ranks at Sam Houston State (Huntsville, Texas), where she was the head basketball coach and in charge of the volleyball and track teams as well.

In 1973, she joined the staff at the University of Texas-Arlington (UTA). Conradt was asked to serve as Athletics Director and to coach basketball, volleyball and softball. Her teams qualified for the national tournaments during her three-year tenure and went 43-39 overall.

In 1976, Conradt arrived at The University of Texas to take over the fledgling programs in basketball and volleyball and wasted no time in charting the path that would lead Texas to unprecedented triumphs. Conradt's successes on the court, visibility in the community and her charismatic nature all helped Texas assemble a major fan base for women's collegiate athletics. In her tenure, nearly 2.3 million fans have watched Texas Basketball live.[3]

Conradt urges young female coaches not to allow anything to overshadow their passion for the game and the opportunities that the game provides. She said, "It's easy to become distracted, to allow other things to become priorities: scholarships, individual recognition, the money, all of those things are great and wonderful by-products, but it still about the love of the game. It's about sharing the love that probably every coach once felt when she played." She also believes that it is the responsibility of all women to recognize the continued achievements of women: "We readily recognize the first woman to do anything. We all stop and salute for the pioneers, but we must continue to salute, recognize, and honor every woman who is successful."

Conradt's lasting footprint on women's basketball may be the number of wins and losses, but she would prefer to be remembered not just as a coach who had great success but as a woman who helped create opportunities for young girls. True she will always remember the championships, but Conradt takes more pride in the fact that every little girl who wants to be a basketball player or who wants to participate in women's sports now can find a way and a place to do that. That doesn't have anything to do with winning or losing. "If I could put anything on my tombstone, it would be 'She Gave Value to Something That No One Saw Value In,'" said Conradt.

Her thoughts turned back to the 1984 team that lost in the

Final Four. "We hosted that Final Four and we didn't play in it. We sold out the arena for the first time in women's Final Four history. Austin, Texas, opened its arms for women's basketball. We were able to sell women's basketball and create a blueprint for other programs to do the same when so many people never believed that would happen. That success gave people hope and a vision. It wasn't just about the wins. It was about being involved in something greater."

Conradt and the dedicated people at the University of Texas took something that the general public did not believe was credible or valuable, and taught the public that it *was* something credible and valuable. It took Conradt a long time to figure out that being so dedicated to the development of the women's game is far more lasting than any championship she could have won.

Shortly after the 2006–7 season concluded, Gail Goestenkors made a change, a huge change. She left the comfort of the thriving Division I, Duke University program in which she had guided the Duke Blue Devils from 1992–93 through the 2006–7 season with an overall record of 396-99 (.800). "It was truly the most difficult decision I have ever made. Ultimately, I remember thinking that I tell my players every day to step out of their comfort zones, to put themselves at risk. I told my team I would be a hypocrite if I weren't willing to do the same things I ask of them. It would be hard for me to look them in the face and know I was taking the safe route. I needed to step out. I see this as a great adventure in my life and it's exciting," Goestenkors said.

While at Duke, Goestenkors never got her hands on that elusive NCAA National Championship title, but she came mighty close more than once. In 2006–7 she led Duke to 32-2 record and to the number-one national ranking in final regular-season polls. She went 29-0 in the regular season, becoming the first Atlantic Coast Conference (ACC) team and only the fourteenth in NCAA history to finish the regular season undefeated. She is the recipient of five 2006–7 National Coach of the Year honors: AP, Naismith, Russell Athletic/Women's Basketball Coaches

Association, USBWA (United States Basketball Writers Association), and ESPN.com. She also received WBCA Regional Coach of the Year and ACC Coach of the Year honors.

Her Duke teams made two NCAA National Championship game appearances (1999, 2006), four NCAA Final Fours (1999, 2002, 2003, 2006), seven NCAA Elite Eight showings (1998, 1999, 2002–6), ten NCAA Sweet Sixteen showings (1998, 1999, 2000–7), plus consecutive NCAA Tournament bids (1995–2007).

As if that's not enough, Goestenkors led Duke to an unprecedented seven consecutive thirty-win seasons from 2000–1 to 2006–7, breaking the mark Duke held along with Louisiana Tech (six straight thirty-plus-win seasons). She led Duke to four NCAA Final Four berths in last nine seasons, eight ACC regular season championships, and five ACC Championship Tournament titles. She's received twelve National Coach of the Year honors, including the Naismith Award and WBCA honor twice (2003, 2007). She's a six-time WBCA District Coach of the Year (1995, 2001–4, 2007) and a seven-time ACC Coach of the Year (1996, 1998, 1999, 2002, 2003, 2004, 2007)—tying Virginia's Debbie Ryan for most ACC Coach of the Year honors. Sure all of those honors and accolades fill up a coach's career stat sheet, but Goestenkors isn't really concerned with her individual honors: "I coach because I'm passionate about the game," she said.

Winning a national championship aside, what really motivates Goestenkors is seeing the light bulb go off in a player's head: "Working with the players appeals most to me. Building relationships with the players has always been my priority. I enjoy watching them learn and grow. When I see the light bulb pop on for them when they understand something or execute something that I'm trying to teach them, I think that's one of the greatest feelings . . . ever." Goestenkors credits her college coach at Saginaw Valley State in Michigan for teaching her the real role of a coach: "I realized how important that relationship is for a student athlete. That's one of the reasons why I got into coaching. It was such a positive experience for me, I just wanted to continue it. If I didn't have a good relationship with my players, I wouldn't coach, that's just too important to me."

All good coaches are good motivators, and Goestenkors is no

different. Like most coaches she uses various tools to motivate her players. At different times players and teams need different things. Part of Goestenkors's secret is to build relationships with her players early-on because every player is motivated in a different way, depending on her personality and her upbringing. "Some players I can yell at. I can get in their faces. Some players won't respond to that and will crumble. Learning what it takes to motivate your individual players and then your team as a whole is so important. Every year with every team, I always say that adversity reveals character. You really find out who you really are when tough times hit," she said.

She also believes that each team has its own distinct personality, and finding the heartbeat and the pulse of a team is really important. For her it's about knowing what her players need in specific situations: "Some teams in a pressure situation need me to be in their faces. Some teams require positive reinforcement to know that they are OK, to understand that they are good enough," Goestenkors said.

Also vital to Goestenkors is self-growth and improvement. She doesn't look at her career numbers with a sense of completion. She looks at her journey as a coach as a steady progression: "I've worked hard to improve every single year. I want my players to improve. I want them to step out of their comfort zone, and I think I've tried to do that as well, particularly with my move to the University of Texas." She also credits USA Basketball for helping her step outside her comfort zone. "In USA Basketball I'm constantly working with college coaches, pro coaches, the best athletes in the world. We travel overseas to many countries where English is not spoken. We're put in tough situations where you have to survive and thrive, which I love," explained Goestenkors. When she comes away from a USA Basketball event, she always comes away knowing she's grown as a person and as a coach, and she hopes to bring those lessons back to her team.

Goestenkors doesn't just talk about basketball. She discusses the game with reverence as if it is a family member who is sitting next to her. For her the game is about the players, the people, the unity and camaraderie, and the relationships she's created as part of playing the game. She recalls playing basketball with her father and brothers in Waterford, Michigan, and those moments are always present. "There are so many magical things about that time for young girls. It's about the one-on-one attention with a parent that's priceless. Then when you are able to play a game you are passionate about, there is such joy in that experience. When you put it all together, it's magic."

To her, basketball is the joy of a great play. She said, "It's the fact that within the two hours of any game at any time, I will go through almost every possible emotion, from joy to anger to fear to excitement and intrigue. There aren't many things you can do in life where in a two-hour time frame you can feel almost every emotion. I love that!"

Goestenkors hit the nail on the head. Basketball does create an environment for virtually every emotion to be played out on a public stage, for all to see. That's always been the draw of sports: its drama unfolding right before our very eyes.

7 The Approach of a Coach

The game of basketball is brutally honest and brutally fair. The best teams win; the best players play. The most talented players go on to play at higher levels. When a mistake is made, it's up on the Jumbo-Tron in instant replay for everyone to see.

Christina Wielgus, head women's basketball coach at Dartmouth College in New Hampshire, thrives in that kind of atmosphere. Dartmouth College is a Division I program, although as an Ivy League school, it does not award athletic scholarships to players as other Division I programs do.

Over the years Wielgus has become to see her role more as a facilitator than as a dictator: "I'm passionate about the game, and I want to teach it to the best of my ability." With ten Ivy League championships, one Patriot League title, and six NCAA

Tournament appearances, Coach Wielgus has established herself as one of the nation's elite coaches. She has proven herself as a big-game coach, leading the Big Green to two consecutive Ivy League Playoff Championships (2005 and 2006) for the league's automatic bid to the NCAA Tournament.

For Wielgus players with the most points or the most accolades don't ensure a winning program. It's really about having a core of people who refuse to lose. It's about creating an expectation of winning, creating a winning tradition that can then be handed down by upperclassmen.

Because Dartmouth doesn't award athletic scholarships, there is the misperception that Dartmouth's student athletes don't have to put forth as much effort as other Division I schools. "Our players work extremely hard, as hard as any other elite program. We just need to do it within the framework of the rules we have been given," said Wielgus. She makes it clear that her players lift just as much and run just as hard: "They shot in their driveways when they were little girls. They grew up around the game. Just because they aren't offered athletic scholarships doesn't make them any less of a player or athlete."

At the 2006 NCAA Tournament, the Big Green put forth a tremendous effort against third-seeded Rutgers. Dartmouth valiantly overcame an 11-point deficit late in the game but eventually fell 63–58 to the Big East Champions. A year later the loss still hurts. Wielgus said, "I still haven't watched the game in its entirety. I only watch the last two minutes over and over and over again. Almost winning is just not the same as winning. Coming from an Ivy League institution facing Rutgers, everyone said, 'Coach, you did, great, you got close.' Well I didn't want to get close. I wanted to win."

"Entering her 23rd season (1976–84, 1993–present) as the head coach of the Big Green, Wielgus has solidified her reputation as one of the top women's basketball strategists in the country. Wielgus is the winningest coach in the illustrious history of Dartmouth College, amassing a stellar record of 330-233 in 22 seasons. Including her two years as a head coach with Fordham, Wielgus sports a 367-254 overall record."[1]

Wielgus attributes her tenure at Dartmouth to one simple

consideration: she still believes she can continue to win year in and year out. The other thing that keeps Wielgus at Dartmouth is how much the women's basketball program is valued there: "We don't have a big arena, but it's filled. There is enormous amount of respect for our work and the quality of play of my athletes, and that's hard to come by."

Her program's progression is proudly noted by Wielgus, who recalls playing in obscurity throughout the 1970s. She not only coached the team, but she also drove the van, did the laundry, and made the sandwiches. Having earned respect over the years at Dartmouth is special for Wielgus. "You know where women earn the respect? Winning. We win when no one else can. We're playing on their field by their rules and we're still winning. The generations of women who played at Dartmouth have earned respect, and I'm proud to be a part of that heritage," she said.

> Wielgus first took over the program in just its fifth year of existence (1976–77) and led the Big Green to unprecedented heights, winning four consecutive Ivy League titles from 1980–83 before leaving Hanover in 1984 after eight seasons. She returned to the College on the Hill prior to the 1993–94 season and has revitalized the most decorated women's basketball program in the Ivy League, leading Dartmouth to six more Ivy League championships and five additional NCAA tournament appearances. During her tenure, Wielgus has created one of the most consistent programs in the Ivies. The Big Green has finished in the top three in the past 17 of 19 seasons."[2]

Thinking back to her earlier years as a coach, Wielgus said, "As a young coach in 1976, I was barely older than the players that I was coaching. When I was young, I thought I knew it all. I used to surround myself with younger people so I would know more than they did. Now when my assistant comes up with something I haven't thought of, I'm beyond excited. Only experience and knowledge about the game has humbled me. The more I've learned about the game, the more I've realized that I don't know that much."

Wielgus's second stint at Dartmouth came after a successful

two-year reign at Fordham University, where the Rams had back-to-back winning seasons for the first time in thirteen years, highlighted by the 1991–92 campaign—Wielgus's first at Rose Hill—when they went 21-8 and won both the Patriot League regular season and the postseason tournament titles.

In between her first Dartmouth stint and her two-year stay at Fordham, Wielgus remained actively involved in women's basketball around the country. She served as training camp coordinator for the United States women's basketball teams that won gold medals at the 1986 Goodwill Games and the 1986 World Championships. Wielgus also directed the Developmental Basketball Program in Hilton Head, South Carolina, and the All-Star Basketball Camps in Baton Rouge, Louisiana and Jacksonville, Florida. Today, she is director of the All-Star Basketball Camp that runs during the summer in Hanover. Wielgus said, "I am absolutely passionate about the game of basketball, and I love what I do. I love teaching it. I love learning it. I still get excited." For her, the beauty of coaching at Dartmouth is that when she enters the gym each day, the student athletes she coaches want to be there. They want to be at practice, and they want to get better. They love the game of basketball, and it shows." For a coach, any coach at any level, it doesn't get much better than that.

The Bear at Practice

Mike McManus was the head women's basketball coach at the Division II, St. Thomas Aquinas College (STAC) program in Sparkill, New York, for twenty-three seasons. He is the winningest coach in STAC history, having eleven twenty-win seasons. He's guided his club to the postseason eighteen times and has advanced three times to the round of sixteen in the National Association of Intercollegiate Athletics (NAIA) Division II tournament. St. Thomas has been a member of NCAA Division II for five years and has been to the NCAA tournament once.

It's easy to miss the STAC campus as one drives down Route 304, very near the Hudson River in New York. The campus is unassuming, with new brick buildings set back from the road housing and educating nearly two thousand students. On a hot summer day the campus was pretty quiet, with only students attending summer classes on campus. After a short walk to the Aquinas Hall Athletic Center, I weaved my way down several narrow stairways to the athletic department offices. Once inside I was introduced to Mike McManus, who sat behind his desk and extended a hand to greet me over a mound of files.

McManus is an imposing presence. He's known for being a tough coach who knows the game extremely well. While many have said that McManus has mellowed over the years, McManus has a different opinion. He hasn't changed so much. It's the student athletes who have changed. McManus's approach has always been the same. He is a firm believer in fundamentals and hard work. If practice is two-hours long, his players are expected to walk in the gym, give everything they have for that practice time and then move on with their days. McManus doesn't believe in constantly checking in on his players. He expects hard work, and he gets it. "I'm a bear at practice, and I think that's where it all begins, at practice. Games come along, and if you've done your homework in practice, things will work out on the court," he said.

Although McManus has been coaching for over two decades, he still enjoys coaching and teaching the game. He explained, "I'm competitive, I like to win. I like game day, and I like what builds up to the win or loss. It's always been what I do. That's why I love working with women. I've coached guys, but women seem to want to learn more, where guys don't care about fundamentals." McManus scoffs at the coaches who treat female players different than male players. He said, "I don't treat women differently because I don't think you can ask for equality and then be treated differently." McManus believes that unlike the men's game, the women's game still revolves below the rim, it still revolves around making the right pass, stepping to the ball, and catching it, so fundamental skills are vital.

He is vocal about the difficulties facing Division II programs, specifically with regard to recruiting and scholarship dollars. He said, "The dedication required at the Division I level is really high. Playing a sport becomes a job, a full-time job. At STAC, and I would assume at most Division II programs, we want our kids to be well rounded. We strictly adhere to the NCAA rules, and we encourage our players to be students outside basketball, be more involved in what's going on. Athletes don't have the time for those additional opportunities at the Division I level."

Erin Kilduff, from Parlin, New Jersey, played for McManus. She said, "My most memorable moments at STAC were playing against Rutgers and Army. Even though we lost, these games were amazing learning experiences for me."

McManus also recalled the game against Rutgers but for a slightly different reason. He said, "A few years ago we were at the 'Rack,' and are standing for the national anthem. One of my kids, a then sophomore from Poughkeepsie is standing next to me. She whispers, 'Hey that's Sue Wicks, she played for the New York Liberty.' That innocent recognition is still relatively new. Even though my player had no clue that Wicks was an All-American at Rutgers, she still recognized her from the WNBA. That's why our sport still needs a professional league."

Corinne Albrecht from Samsonville, New York, sat out her first season at St. Thomas because of a blown-out shoulder. She told me that she loves the game because it helps her find her own sense of self: "Every day going on the court to work hard and better myself and my team is rewarding. I have something to look forward to every day. In the big picture, working towards a championship is a goal that's hard to reach. It takes dedication and hard work. I love to work hard for something meaningful. That is why I play. Basketball teaches you to keep your head up."

Albrecht laughed at her own remarks, recalling her first college memory at STAC: "Although it is hard to keep your head up when you've been elbowed in the eye. My first college game memory was when we played the University of Bridgeport, and I got elbowed in the head. I was knocked out and had a black eye. I think of this now because that moment motivated me to play harder and be tougher." Black eye or not, you've got to keep your head up. Any coach will tell you that as they apply the ice to your swollen cheek.

Coaching in the City That Never Sleeps

Make no mistake about it, Janice Quinn is just about as intense a coach as one will find at any level. She has been New York

University's head women's basketball coach for the past twenty-one seasons, establishing herself as one of the top coaches in the country. New York University, a Division III program, cannot award athletic scholarships to student athletes.

In each of the seasons Quinn has coached, her teams have posted winning records, earning her Hall of Fame honors. Her Violets have won at least twenty games sixteen times, including thirteen consecutive seasons, 1992–93 to 2004–5. Quinn's teams have produced a 439-116 (.791) overall record. Even still, her desire to win is still amazingly passionate.

Coach Quinn said, "I'd say if you're coaching for over twenty years and your approach hasn't changed, then you're not doing a very good job because you're spanning two decades, and the kids have definitely changed." Similar to Dianne Nolan from Fairfield University, Quinn cites that the mindset of an eighteen- to twenty-two-year-old college student is markedly different. She said, "It's different because their sense of society and their sense of themselves in society is different than it was. The ways in which I teach those values are obviously impacted by the society these kids are in. What used to be certain methods of getting their attention and of appealing to a certain mindset is very different than it was a decade or even two decades ago because society has changed."

Quinn believes that the typical member of the American society, whether college-aged or adult, has a greater sense of entitlement now. "This generation has more of a sense of entitlement than generations before, and I'm from one of those generations before. The ability to connect with a student athlete is a continuous and dynamic challenge," said Quinn. For her it's imperative that she be able to get through to her student athletes in ways they can value: "It's just a matter of just packaging the message in a more appropriate way because when it's packaged the right way, using the right method, I can reach these young people with the same intensity."

Certain aspects of Quinn's coaching have remained exactly the same. Buzzwords such as hard work, discipline, attention to detail, working within a unit, competitiveness, and desire are the foundations of her program and her core beliefs about coaching. "The x's and o's have changed a ton. My approach to the game has evolved. The women's game has certainly evolved dramatically in the last fifteen to twenty years. The overall competition level in women's basketball has increased. There is so much more talent out there, so there's a lot more parity," said Quinn.

After assuming the NYU head coach position in 1987 following four years as a player and two years as an assistant, Quinn immediately stated one simple goal: to win the national championship. In 1997, she made good on that vow.

In Quinn's first year as head coach (1987–88), the team set a then-school record with 21 wins. Her second team was 18-9, advanced to the NCAA Sweet Sixteen, and grabbed a three-way share of first-place in the UAA [University Athletic Association]. In '94–95, Quinn took an inexperienced, injury-riddled team to a 23-5 record. With the women's NCAA Tournament expanded to 64 teams, the Violets won two tournament games to reach the Sweet Sixteen for the third consecutive year. The Metropolitan Basketball Writers' Association honored her as their 1994–95 Division III Coach of the Year.

The '95–96 Violets reeled off four NCAA Tournament wins and advanced to the Final Four before losing to eventual national champion University of Wisconsin-Oshkosh. That squad was the first NYU women's team to reach the Final Four. Quinn and her assistants were named UAA Co-Coaching Staff of the Year. Quinn was also named Columbus Multimedia East Region Coach of the Year and Metropolitan Basketball Writers' Division III Coach of the Year.

In a career full of highlights, the 1996–97 championship season stands out among the rest. That year, the Violets capped off a near-perfect 29-1 (.967) season with a thrilling, 72–70, buzzer-beater to win in the National Title game over the University of Wisconsin-Eau Claire. Quinn received Coach of the Year accolades from *Women's Division III News*, the Metropolitan Basketball Writers' Association and the Converse Basketball Coaches' Association of New York. Quinn and her assistants were also named UAA Coaching Staff of the Year.[3]

"The road to the national championship will always stand out as a highlight of my journey here at NYU," Quinn revealed.

Quinn's Violets followed up their national championship season with a 22-5 record in 1997–98, advancing to the NCAA Sweet Sixteen for the sixth consecutive season. In 1998–99 the Violets advanced to the NCAA Elite Eight and set a Division III record in the process with their seventh consecutive appearance in the Sweet Sixteen. That squad finished with a 24-4 overall record, including a 12-2 UAA mark.

In 2001–2 the Bay Shore, New York, native led the Violets to a 26-2 record (including thirteen straight wins to begin the season), the UAA Co-Championship, and another appearance in the Elite Eight. The Metropolitan Basketball Writers' Association again named Quinn Division III Women's Coach of the Year, and Quinn recorded her milestone 300th career win on February 13, 2001, versus York College (79–55). She is now nearing career win 450.

"The [2001] squad overcame a great deal more adversity than a 26-2 record would indicate. For that I am quite proud," Quinn said. "Reaching the Elite Eight four times in a six-year span is quite an accomplishment. Defeating the national champions (Washington University) in the regular season and capturing a share of the UAA title really stood out as highlights of that season."

In 2003–4 the Violets finished with a 23-4 record, won the UAA Co-Championship, and advanced to the NCAA Tournament Sweet Sixteen. Quinn and her assistants were named UAA Coaching Staff of the Year, while she was also awarded Metropolitan Basketball Writers' Association Division III Coach of the Year honors for the third time in seven seasons.

In 2005–6 the Violets finished 18-8 overall, 7-7 in the UAA, and earned their twelfth NCAA Tournament bid during the Quinn era.

The 2006–2007 season was another stellar season for Quinn, again illustrating the culture of excellence she has created at NYU. Reaching the NCAA Division III Sweet 16 for the first time since 2004, the Violets capped off their season with an overall record of 27-4, and an 18-0 unbeaten home record, a feat rarely matched in Division III. Quinn was also named D3Hoops.com East Region and NYSWCAA [New York State Women's Collegiate Athletic Association] Coach of the Year. She earned the Metropolitan Basketball Writers' Association (MBWA) Women's College Basketball Coach of the Year Award, and led NYU to tie for its second most victories ever, win its sixth UAA title and reach the NCAA Division III Tournament for the 11th time.[4]

From the very beginning of her association with NYU, Quinn began leaving an indelible mark. As a junior in 1983–84, she captained her teammates to a 16-10 record (the school's first winning record since 1961–62), following a 7-16 mark the year before. The next year Quinn was named the team's MVP and Best All-Around Player as the Violets recorded their first-ever twenty-win season (20-9).

When her playing career ended, Quinn had become the first 1,000-point scorer (1,137) in the history of the women's program at New York University. She graduated with honors in economics in 1985 and went on to earn a master's degree in finance from NYU's Wagner School of Public Service and the Stern School of Business.

Quinn discussed her perspective on the women's game this way: "I've been in college basketball for a long, long time. I have been in college basketball going on my twenty-seventh year: four years as a player, two years as an assistant, and twenty-one years as a head coach. I've also been an administrator for twenty-one years, so I have a perspective of not just basketball but of other sports as well." Quinn's belief is that a gym is just a gym. All across the country are coaches working to make their players better. Men and women, girls and boys, the game is still the game. For Quinn coaching is simply coaching. The high-school coach in Florida, the junior-college coach in Wisconsin, the Division III coach in New York City all walk into the gym the same way: "Pat Summitt, Bobby Knight, Mike Krzyzewski, and Billy Donovan don't treat what's going on at NYU as any different than what's going on at their campuses because there is that common thread of basketball."

Quinn is the winningest coach in NYU women's basketball history. The NYU teams she has been associated with have recorded all sixteen of the University's twenty-win seasons and have made all of its fourteen NCAA Division III Tournament appearances. These are big numbers for any NCAA division, illustrating that at the Division III level, there are many exceptional student athletes. The generalization that the elite athletes play Division I, while those athletes who simply love the game play at the Division III level still irks Quinn. She said, "I take exception to the mindset that generally Division III players only because they love it, not because they are extremely talented athletes."

Quinn explained, "If you're talking about big-time Division I like the Tennessees and UConns, those are the elite athletes, no question, but when you get out of the top twenty, I think the lines between really high level Division III and Division I, to me, are nonexistent. The top level Division I athletes possess four distinct traits: great athleticism, great skill, great desire, and great love. At the highest level in Division II and Division III, players still possess all four attributes, although they possess those attributes to a slightly lower degree. I've had some kids that could have played anywhere in Division I. Maybe they couldn't have played at Tennessee, but they could have played for almost everybody else."

Quinn added, "Too many people make broad-sweeping statements about Division I and Division III, and I think they're wrong about both. The concept that the kids in Division III just play because they love it I think is dead wrong. The concept that Division I only has the elite athletes is dead wrong. When you get outside of top twenty, I don't think the lines are as clearly delineated as some people may think."

A ten-time Metropolitan Basketball Writers' Association Coach of the Year and four-time New York State Women's Collegiate Athletic Association Coach of the Year, Quinn was also honored in 1998 as the Metropolitan Basketball Officials' Association Sportsman of the Year.

Quinn still loves to talk x's and o's with just about anyone. She loves the challenge of getting fifteen people to a strategic point that they understand and can implement. "I get a great deal of satisfaction in the implementation of a drill in and of itself. By the same token, when a practice doesn't go well, I take a great deal of responsibility for that. I generally feel that if practice doesn't go well, it probably wasn't constructed well," said Quinn. Her success hinges on teaching the right items for the team at the right time and place. According to Quinn, a particular practice on paper might be a great practice for a Saturday afternoon, but on a particular Tuesday in December, that might be the totally wrong practice to have, based on fatigue, based on timing, based the mindset of the team.

She said, "I find it enormously rewarding to get 15 people on the same page. The most satisfying thing that I do is finding with the right words to help one of my student athletes perform better." That, for Quinn, is a constant challenge.

Adrienne Rochetti, a New Jersey native, played for Coach Quinn. Quinn described Rochetti as "being an undersized kid with major Division I skills." In high school Rochetti averaged 19 points, 5 assists, and 4 steals per game as a senior. She broke the Sacred Heart and Cumberland County scoring records with 1,913 career points, helped lead her team to a 27-2 record and the New Jersey state championship as a senior, and was named All-South Jersey in both basketball and tennis, as well as serving as the salutatorian of her senior class.

Rochetti said, "My passion and love for the game of basketball is so strong that it's difficult to put into words. In the most pure and simple sense, I love the way it feels to play the game. I love the way the ball feels in my hand when I dribble or the way a jump shot feels when I've achieved the perfect back spin and know that I am about to hear 'swish.' On a deeper level, I love the game because I see it as a form of expression and entertainment." Rochetti told me that she is a fairly shy person off the court, so basketball has always been her way to reveal herself to the outside world. Basketball is her vehicle to show the heart, fight, and passion that burn inside of her. "I love this game because it's taught me countless lessons about myself and allowed me to truly test the growth that I have made in my life off the court," said Rochetti.

Rochetti admits that it seems strange, but she can remember details of every game she has ever played in since the fifth grade when she began her CYO career. She recalls winning the state championship her senior year of high school: "It was so special because we were major underdogs, and we were down by thirteen points going into the fourth quarter. The atmosphere was unbelievable."

Now when she looks back at high school and thinks about her college career, she easily remembers the glamorous moments such as beating high-ranked teams or playing in the Sweet Sixteen, but the big moments don't stand out any more to her than executing a perfect fast break at practice. "I realize that I love it all the same. The feeling is generated from the energy and love of my teammates and coaches. I get the chills when I think about what it feels like to be carried by the collective spirit of my team here at NYU. I can feel that spirit too in an empty gym during a long and draining practice. Coach Quinn taught me that kind of intensity," Rochetti concluded.

"Obviously, I've coached for over twenty years," explained Quinn, "so there's a lot I like about it. It's very difficult for me to separate my job from my alma mater, from my city, from my home—they're all the same." Hers is a unique perspective, and Quinn definitely appreciates it.

Quinn loves that she coaches at her alma mater—that connection still means a great deal. "I don't think I would love coaching as much if it were not at my alma mater. New York is my hometown, my home city. Those are important things to me. My players are doing exactly what I did. They walk the same halls; they're taking the same courses and experiencing the same challenges of college life in New York City," she said. That continuum of past, present, and future is still satisfying and exciting to this coach. She admits not very much in life stays the same. Certainly nothing in New York stays the same for very long. Yet in the middle of this very dynamic and changing environment, this is still Quinn's home base.

Coaches Weilgus, McManus, and Quinn all exude a passion about the game that's nearly impossible to miss. The only thing that separates them is the NCAA division in which they play.

With the lines blurred, each is a teacher, a facilitator, a sports psychologist, a mentor, and a disciplinarian. Each coach wants to motivate his or her team to perform at the highest possible level. Perfection is rarely reached in basketball, but these coaches get up every day with perfection in mind.

8 A Dance Is Still a Dance

When most basketball fans think of college hoops, they immediately call to mind the NCAA Division I tournament, the field of sixty-four, the Cinderella stories and the Big Dance, the underdogs and the Kameron Crazies.

However, the vast majority of NCAA basketball players don't ever get the opportunity to play in the national tournament. Most of these players do experience conference tournaments and close games, but rarely is there a television camera to capture the buzzer beater or the clutch free throws down the stretch.

Playing Division III basketball at Mount Saint Mary College (MSMC) in Newburgh, New York, was an absolute joy for me. As reflected in its motto "Doce Me Veritatem" (Teach me the truth), Mount Saint Mary College, founded by the Dominican

Sisters of Newburgh in 1930, is an independent coeducational institution committed to providing students with a liberal arts education.

I realized many years later how absolutely blessed I was to have spent four years focused on the game I so love. College athletes and college students across the country develop strong ties with their alma maters, which usually last a lifetime. Not many people have ever heard of Mount Saint Mary College, but that doesn't matter much to me. It's still a place I call home.

My most memorable college game came in my senior season at MSMC against one of our biggest rivals, Vassar College.

Coach's halftime speeches were never a thing of beauty. He rarely spoke in complete sentences without a curse. He usually spit when he spoke, and depending on how angry he was, one or two garbage cans might be tossed into different corners. Some days he was inspiring; others, it was a torment just to keep a straight face.

"C'mon now. For chrissakes, what happened out there? We've successfully blown a twelve-point lead, and now we're only up two. You look like a bunch of drunks. Jamie, I haven't seen you set a screen since last week at practice. Move your feet and just once tonight, try to make contact with the person you're sup-posed to be picking, OK? Kristie, shoot the three if you're open. You're buck-naked at the top of the key, and you're passing to Kelly, who has three people around her. I haven't even seen any semblance of a goddamned play the last three minutes. Now Jesus, pull yourselves together. Look around. They're not that good. You're just letting them think they are. When we go out, twenty-two defense. Shut down their perimeter. Liz, see if you can pick the ball off when they swing cross-court. Be ready to help her. Ladies, you've got twenty minutes left in this one. Don't blow it. Get out there and finish them off."

The first nineteen minutes of the second half were not a thing of beauty either. Because we had let Vassar back into the game in the first half, they were pumped and willing to trade buckets with us down the stretch. Their pressure was stifling, and we turned the ball over far more than we should have. We were playing on Vassar's home floor, and their fans provided an additional safety net that propelled them into a tie game with fifty-three seconds remaining.

Coach called a time-out to set us up for the next offensive possession. Walking back onto the court following the timeout I thought, *If I could just get the ball in the corner, I'm wide open there. Kristie can't see me because she's so damned short. OK, this is it. Ankle hurts badly. Ignore it. You can ignore anything. Where's dad? There he is in that blue shirt. If he has that shirt on, it means we'll win. What play are we running? We're running Circle. Get to the opposite post. Get ready, number twenty-four is going to hit you.*

Whistle blows. Jamie, a six-foot forward, is waiting for Trenetta to slap the ball out of bounds, setting the play in motion. We hear the slap, and Jamie goes in motion. She's rushing, going too fast, circles in and misses her first screen. Kelly, a shorter than average but lightning quick two guard, is supposed to come off the screen Jamie sets, but since the screen is nonexistent, she can't get free. Liz rushes up to help get the ball in-bounds, wants to set another screen to get Kelly free, but doesn't get there in time. Liz is blessed with a pure shooter's touch, not foot speed, and even less foot speed with a severe case of shin splints.

From my vantage point near the corner, I can hear the squeak of Liz's sneakers. With every step, she's wincing in pain from her shin splints, but only fifty-three seconds left, she too deals with the pain. I can feel the sweat from my legs soaked into the athletic tape on my left ankle—it's itchy and cold against my skin. Number twenty-four on the other team holds Liz's shirt, and her neck snaps back. The referee misses this, and Liz stares down the official as she rushes by the black-and-white striped shirt. *If she cuts left, I can get free and get the ball.* The out-of-bounds official's left arm has come down three times, four times. "CALL TIMEOUT, JAMIE!" screams Coach. Whistle blows. "Violation white, red ball," shouts the official.

Coach's tie is just about off. I can see the sweat on his upper lip and know he's angry because his forehead turned bright red. He grabs Jamie as she's running down-court and yells in her face, "Get your goddamned head in this game right now, or you'll spend what's left of this season and some of next season sitting next to me. You got that?" Jamie winces as spit flies on her face as she breaks free and continues to run down-court.

The Vassar point guard reminds her team that we'll be doubling down in the corner. She says, "Shelly, come up-court right and swing me the ball once you get over half court." Vassar's point guard is good. She wipes her sweaty hands on her navy jersey that looks black with her sweat soaked entirely through and brings the ball up-court. She glances over at the coach, who looks calm and collected on the bench. Our defense rushes out and attacks her at midcourt. She turns her back swiftly and spins the other direction firing a bullet chest pass to her teammate who is waiting with her hands ready to catch and release. It's a perfectly thrown pass and a technically perfect shot. The ball goes through the hoop, and I take it out of the net to take the ball back out of bounds. We're now down two with twenty-six seconds remaining in the game. I'm surprised there is no full-court press by Vassar and easily inbound to Kristie. Kristie runs the ball across half court to Coach and calls timeout.

I don't recall much about that timeout except Coach kept reminding us it was our last one. He draws up a play that doesn't look like much to me and tells us to foul immediately should we lose possession without scoring. Kristie and I, the two seniors and captains on the team, lock eyes with one another and right then, I know we will win. We prepare to inbound and notice immediately that Vassar is in a two-three zone. This surprises us a little since we drew up the play against man-to-man. Good move by the Vassar coach, who knows we can't call timeout to talk it over. Coach starts screaming for a zone play instead.

Kristie should pass to the wing and cut through the center. Instead, she drives. Twenty-two seconds left. The lane closes up and Kristie backs out. *Where is Liz? In the corner. We can't get it to her there.* "Liz, swing through," Kelly yells. Liz can't hear her over the noise and doesn't move. It looks like her feet are cemented to the floor. Kristie passes to Kelly on the right wing. Kelly fakes a shot, but the Vassar defense is too smart to leave Kelly open. She's already burned them for seventeen points. Kristie barrels down the lane and sets a monster pick on the defender guarding the left wing. This allows me to swing up to the left wing and receive a clear pass from Kelly. Kelly in turn goes down the lane without the ball and tries to free up Jamie inside. Valuable time is ticking away. The shot clock is off and eight seconds remain in the game.

Jamie somehow is able to get in front of her defender, thanks to some strong footwork in the lane. She posts hard, and I get her the ball on the left block. She's swarmed. I fade farther down the left wing, behind the three-point line. Time stops. I hear nothing. I see only the ball, the basket, and the clock above the rim ticking silently down. With three seconds left, Jamie somehow squeezes the ball out of the lane to me. But it's a bad pass, and I'm sliding to my left toward the baseline to regain possession. I don't think; I simply react. I track the ball down, set my feet, and shoot the ball, falling out of bounds after I release it. When I hit the ground, I feel the pain in my left ankle and know I rolled it again. Nothing keeps my eyes from that never-ending jump shot. It sails in the air for what feels like hours. I hear the buzzer sound. The ball is still in the air, and every person on the court has turned into a still life. No one dares to move. I close my eyes. In that split second, I hear it. I hear the sound I love more than any other: the sound of leather hitting cotton, the sound of a perfect shot. It is the sound of victory.

At least, that's the way I remember it.

Randy Ognibene is still the head coach of the Mount Saint Mary College Blue Knights. Entering his eighteenth season as the head coach, Ognibene is one of the most successful Division III basketball coaches of all time. He ranks fourteenth among all NCAA Division III basketball coaches for victories, having amassed 441 victories in his twenty-six-year career. While at Mount Saint Mary College, Ognibene is 333-99 and has led his team to seven straight appearances at the NCAA Division III tournament.

The Blue Knights have averaged nearly twenty-one wins per season under Ognibene's watch and have hit the twenty-win plateau ten times in the last eleven seasons. In addition Ognibene has guided the Mount to five Eastern Collegiate Athletic Conference (ECAC) tournament appearances, one ECAC championship in 1997–98, and three second-place finishes in the ECAC tournament.

Since 1999–2000, Ognibene has led the Blue Knights to seven straight NCAA Division III Championships appearances, seven Skyline Conference titles, and three second-place finishes at the New York State Women's Collegiate Athletic Association Tournament. Mount Saint Mary has also advanced to the second round of the NCAA tourney two times — once in 2000–1 and once in 2004–5.

Ognibene has accrued a staggering 66-1 record within the Skyline Conference. He has won outright or shared Skyline Conference Coach of the Year honors in each of the past seven seasons. Ognibene was also named the Women's Intercollegiate Athletic Conference Coach of the Year in 1992–93 and 1995–96.

As his former player and fan of his program, I've watched Ognibene over the years and definitely think he's mellowed. His response is, "I'm not more mellow. I still want to win; I just don't yell as much anymore." Ognibene realized that if he yelled all the time, his players just tuned him out and stopped listening. "They can't pick out what's really important. At some point I just smartened up and realized that most of the time, the players are really trying to please their coach and do what's asked of them, but they make some mistakes as we all do. Yelling just makes their performance worse. I've learned to pick my spots and pick my targets carefully." When I began coaching high school again two years ago, he allowed me to sit in his practices. He sent me his playbook and helped prepare me for life as a coach, and with his help, I have become a better coach.

A few years ago, I received a call from the sports information director at MSMC. They were cleaning out the trophy cases and asked if I wanted my all-time leading scorer's ball and a few other items of achievement from my time at MSMC. In addition to making me feel old, that call made me proud because I knew it meant that the MSMC women's basketball program was growing, which made me feel good to have once been a part of it.

Shannon Sangster from Syracuse, New York, plays for Coach Ognibene as I once did. Sangster said the adjustment to college basketball from high school was tough. "The intensity level is so much higher. In high school, we were good, but our practices weren't nearly as intense. In high school, I had girls on my team who played just because it was convenient to, not because they really loved the game. Practices at Mount Saint Mary College are so much more intense. Here everyone gives 100 percent at practice, and I wasn't used to that. I thought I knew basketball before I came here, but I've learned so much. Every day, the little things that they say, I'll remember and try to use that in a game situation."

Chrissy Zrowka from Brick, New Jersey, also played for the Mount Saint Mary College Blue Knights. She told me that it's the competition she enjoys the most. Zrowka explained, "For me, it's the competition. It's the high you get off of winning a big game. I love being an underdog and coming in to beat a good team. I've wanted to play basketball for as long as I can remember. When I was in fourth grade, I played in a fifth- and-sixth-grade league. I was the point guard, and I was dribbling up-court and had the ball stolen from me twice in a row. I didn't want to bring it up anymore, but my coach told me I had to. So I did, and I got by my defender with this behind the back dribble. I made a quick pass and my teammate made a shot."

Sangster cut in to ask her teammate incredulously, "You did a behind the back dribble in fourth grade?"

Zrowka replied, laughing, "Yeah, I did. I was so excited. That's when I realized I was pretty good."

They say that if you are called to be a coach, it means you were taught to love the game by someone who coached you. I cannot think of a better compliment to Coach Ognibene. He made me want to be a better coach.

Part four The WNBA

9 Over Ten Years and Going Strong in the WNBA

When I was a freshman at Mount Saint Mary College, I often snuck into the gym when the Kaplan Athletic Center was closed for the night. Noah, the head janitor, was usually on his last leg of cleaning the foyer floors. I sat at midcourt, facing one basket or another fascinated with the way the rim left shadows on the court. Other times I shot around with the first basketball I'd ever owned as a child. The grips on this ball were entirely worn off, and it was as smooth and slippery as a wet fish. To hear the solitary basketball dance with me and the hardwood, dance in my hands, and dance in the air was as close to perfection as I thought I'd ever get.

The last time I snuck into the Kaplan Recreation Facility, I was a senior and our season had just ended. It was after one o'clock in the morning when Noah let me in, patting me on the back. The Pepsi scoreboard lights were on, as always, and they cast a comforting red and blue glow on the court.

Continuing my ritual, I sat at midcourt and picked a basket to face. I closed my eyes and this time, I remembered the game I hit the winning shot with only two seconds left on the clock. I felt the energy and I heard the applause. I closed my eyes and saw myself running down-court with the number fifteen on the back of my gold and royal blue uniform. I thought about the jokes, friendships, and the moments when we were too sore to lift our arms, when we didn't think we could sprint another step but continued to run hard anyway.

When I graduated from college in 1995, I had the opportunity to play professional basketball in Israel. I declined because at the time I was completely burned out. I was also fearful that the only thing I would ever be good at would be confined to inside the lines of the court.

For the first six months or so after graduation from college, I loved my new freedom away from the game. I had made a decision, and it was time to stick to it. For the first time in my life, my afternoons and evenings were wide-open, without three-hour practices. I realized how many other activities I had been unable to experience because all of my spare time had been spent on the court. I kayaked, took up jogging outside, did anything but play basketball. I let myself gain some perspective on life beyond the baseline.

That September I traveled through Europe with one of my closest friends. In that month away I almost forgot about pre-season. I almost forgot the echo of a ball on an empty court. Almost. In Italy when I walked down the street toward the Trevi Fountain, a stranger didn't see an athlete or a basketball player, he saw a young woman. I wasn't quite certain how I felt about that since a basketball player was all I had ever really been.

When I returned in October, I began a new job in a small public-relations agency. I officially entered what jaded cynics call the "real world." Working in a windowless, airless, hoop-less office for thirteen hours a day didn't help that transition much either.

The following year the WNBA launched its inaugural season. In 1997 the fledgling league announced open tryouts at Emory University in Georgia. I decided it was worth a shot. I went to my old grammar school and told them I needed a place to work out. They gave me keys to their gym and told me I could use it any evening after six o'clock. It was an old, musty smelling basement with small dirt covered windows near the ceiling. When I was in sixth and seventh grade, I loved this gym. I thought it was plenty big and the best possible place I could spend my time. The floor was an old hardwood one with plenty of hollow spots. About ten inches separated the end lines from the outer walls with no protective pads in sight. A small stage took up the open space on the right baseline.

For my first practice I changed out of my work clothes in the small, grammar-school-size bathrooms. I waited at least twenty minutes for the lights to warm up and illuminate the court. I stretched and began to do the warm-up drills I had done thousands of times in the past. The gym was totally silent except for my sneakers squeaking against the hardwood, my grunts, my dribbling and shooting. I ran suicides. I timed myself for Mikan drills (lay-up drills designed by NBA great George Mikan) and took over five hundred shots that first night in the empty gym.

I continued to work out like this for several weeks, two or three hours a day. While I felt myself getting stronger, while I experienced the satisfaction of pushing my body and feeling my muscles respond, I was alone on the court each and every night. Basketball is not a solitary sport. It's a team sport and much of the enjoyment revolves around the interaction with your teammates. I recognized I needed to find a league or at least some pickup games. The local leagues had all ended for the winter and the summer leagues had not yet begun. The college and high-school seasons were wrapping up, so I couldn't even practice with some local teams. I was a basketball orphan. Even though I continued to practice silently and alone in the hopes of a tryout, I knew I wouldn't stand a chance if I couldn't get some serious hours of playing time under my belt.

When the letter came in the mail confirming my attendance

for the open tryout, I tore it up and threw it away. I gave the keys back to the grammar-school secretary. I went back to my job, willing myself to put the game behind me. I knew I wasn't ready for a professional tryout, and I refused to embarrass myself. The weekend of the tryout, I drove to Massachusetts and found a quaint little bed and breakfast. Alone, I thought about where I had been and where I was going. I understood that life had more to offer me off the court now, and I had to force those pipe dreams as far away as I could if I was going to be successful. That weekend alone in Massachusetts, I forced myself to come to terms with the fact that I had missed the window. Humans are creatures of habit. We have our daily rituals and our weekly routines. For the most part we go about them all with a quiet vague sense of timing and satisfaction, or dissatisfaction as the case may often be.

Eighteen years of organized basketball had ended, eighteen years of practices and singing the national anthem off-key before every contest. When I was in the middle of those eighteen years, I took the game for granted. I bickered and I complained. Complaints or not, the game was always there woven into the fabric of all I was to become.

It never occurred to me that I was one of a growing number of former female basketball players turned consumers. I never considered the possibility that the WNBA would not succeed or that I was one of a growing market that the WNBA marketing professionals would hope to reach. I also never had many friends who were not sports fans. My male friends did not differentiate between men's sports and women's sports. If you could play, it didn't matter whether you were a boy or a girl. My female friends were sports fanatics like me. It didn't matter if we watched golf or beach volleyball or women's basketball; sports are sports and fun to watch.

When the WNBA launched in 1996, many expected the league to fail, as several of its predecessors had done. Clay Kallam from *Full Court Press* wrote in his article "The WNBA at Age 10" that "of course, there were bumps along the way, and there are bruises ahead, but after 10 years, the WNBA is firmly planted in the American sporting consciousness."[1] Kallam believed the league had history and tradition. "There are rivalries, there are heroes, there are villains. There have been dynasties, and there are legends," he said. He also pointed to franchises that had remained in the same city for over a decade because they are now part of the sporting scene. On a larger scale Kallam believes that young female basketball players from all over the country have WNBA dreams: "Unlike their elders, they don't doubt its survival; to the younger generation, it's as solid as the NBA or the NFL."[2]

The 2006 WNBA Finals, which aired live on ESPN2, saw the Detroit Shock top the Sacramento Monarchs in the first WNBA Finals matchup ever to reach a fifth and deciding game. According to the WNBA, the average attendance for the 2006 Finals was up 28 percent compared to the year before, while average attendance for the playoffs overall increased by 16 percent. The historic Game 5 featured a sellout crowd of 19,671 at Joe Louis Arena in Detroit, Michigan, the second largest crowd in WNBA Finals history. These increases followed closely on the heels of a strong second half of the regular season in which attendance throughout the league rose nearly 12 percent after the All-Star Break.

The WNBA also noted that television viewership increased during the Finals. Detroit's game four win at Sacramento was the second-most watched WNBA game in ESPN2 history, with average viewership for the 2006 Finals up 11 percent over that of 2005. As the preeminent women's sports league, the WNBA, which features thirteen teams, is the destination for the best women's basketball players in the world.

Roughly 160 women play in the WNBA. According to the University of Central Florida's 2004 *Race and Gender Report Card* (RGRC), in the 2004 WNBA season, 33 percent of the players were white, 66 percent were African American (an all-time high), and 1 percent were Latina. Sixteen percent of the players were international. There was a 5 percent increase for African American players in the league and a 2 percent decrease for white players. Among all the professional leagues covered in the RGRC, the WNBA league office had the highest percentages of people of color (40 percent) and women (90 percent) in professional positions.[3]

Nearly 50 million women (roughly one-third of all U.S. women) avidly follow professional sports according to a 2002 national study from Scarborough Sports Marketing.[4] There is no doubt that women control the majority of the buying power when it comes to sports apparel and footwear related items. Between 1997 and 2000 the sales of women's sports apparel rose 20 percent to $15.9 billion, while men's spending inched up just 1 percent to $15.1 billion, according to NPD Group, a marketing research firm, and the Sporting Goods Manufacturers Association. Even more important, women spend 80 percent of all sports apparel dollars, based on NPD data.[5]

Approximately 60 million people watched WNBA games or programming in 2002. Women make up 47.2 percent of Major League Soccer's fans, 46.5 percent of Major League Baseball's, 43.2 percent of the National Football League's, 40.8 percent of the National Hockey League's, and 37 percent of the National Basketball Association's.[6] In 2001 women composed about one-third (34 percent) of the adult audience for ESPN sport event programs. In older groups a larger percentage of the audience is composed of women: those eighteen to thirty-four (31 percent), thirty-five to fifty-four (32 percent), fifty-five plus (40 percent). In 1999, 59 percent of females and 27 percent of males felt better about purchasing products or services from a company that sponsored/supported women's sports.[7]

These statistics illustrate that women are already playing a major role as sports fans and as consumers. According to Leslie Heywood and Shari Dworkin in their book titled *Built to Win: The Female Athlete as Cultural Icon*, "The rise of the female athlete as icon was also partially the result of a shift in attention to the status and condition of girls in America and their cultivation as a consumer market."[8] Yet with all the progress in participation and interest in athletics, mass market appeal to the female athlete is relatively new. Athletes, coaches, administrators, and marketers must navigate an extremely competitive sport and entertainment landscape to find solid footing for women's sports. According to ESPN, 70 to 75 percent of the television audience is male. Globally this difficulty is magnified by cultural, social, and religious differences and belief systems in the way females and female athletes are perceived and ultimately embraced. "It's all part of social roles, too," said Northern Arizona University sociology professor Doug Degher. "If you look at something as banal as Thanksgiving dinner, women are in the kitchen, it doesn't matter if they're liberated or not."[9]

Certainly incredible successes such as the 1999 Women's World Cup Soccer Team and the 1996 Women's Olympic Basketball team had significant impacts in the female athlete iconography. As a result of those successes, Scott Salinardi stated in his article titled "She's Got Game: Women's Interest in Sports Grows Significantly" that women's fan participation was "catapulted to new levels, but equally important, marketers began to realize the potential power of the female fan base."[10]

Kristin Bernert, senior director, team business development at the WNBA, works with the teams on all aspects of their business. She also serves as a liaison between the league and the teams. She said, "The goals for marketing are always to sell more tickets. We have very affordable prices, even in the lower bowl. People can watch some of the best athletes in the world for less than the price of a movie ticket."

It's clear that the WNBA wants to have a united voice as to who they are. "Whether you attend a game, meet a player, or just think about the WNBA, there is one word we all agree on: 'inspirational,'" said Bernert. "We are a basketball league, an incredibly inspirational basketball league. As long as we communicate that in all of our marketing efforts over time, the message will resonate with people. People want to be a part of something inspirational. You can immediately feel that energy when you attend a game."

Donna Lopiano believes the WNBA is in the healthiest position that it could possibly be in. She said, "A new business, especially one that is operating at that level, needs people with an appetite to stay in it for the long term without profit. I think that's one good piece of the puzzle." Lopiano also acknowledged that the WNBA started up in the strongest possible way and did not make the mistake of the Women's United Soccer Association because the WNBA used existing grassroots marketing machines and venue contracts. For the WNBA, this meant not needing to develop an infrastructure in order to start the league. With the NBA leadership and David Stern behind the WNBA, Lopiano likes what she sees in terms of the WNBA.

Lopiano does address two areas of concern that are holding the WNBA back. First is coverage by television with adequate promotion and a good and predictable timeslot. "Nobody has it, nobody can get it," said Lopiano. That goes for men's minor sports too because of the clutter and the dominance of the 'Big Four' television entities. According to Lopiano, the delivery systems have sold their souls with exorbitant rights fees, and until either the digital universe makes appointment viewing a reality or another promotional mechanism is uncovered, it's a very difficult situation for any women's professional sport to break through.

"The other piece of the puzzle is promotion," Lopiano said." Even if you're not on television, you must spend money on promotion in order to get the crowds necessary to sustain the league in a meaningful way. The media coverage on the sports pages is a very significant promotional tool that you don't have to buy. If that coverage isn't there, it's a problem."

In reference to Game 5 of the WNBA Finals on September 9, 2006, Kristen Bernert from the WNBA commented on the atmosphere at that game: "It's always so inspiring to go into an environment like that. When you see the line of people literally across a bridge and down a parking deck waiting to enter the arena, it's a thing of beauty. To see the fans with their handmade signs, dressed to support their favorite team, screaming at the top of their lungs as they react to every play, that's what the WNBA is all about. We have such active fans. When you get an arena full of them, it's a ton of fun."

Bernert believes that basketball brings people together of all races, backgrounds, and all walks of life like no other sport ever has or ever will. "It does not matter where you came from. All you need is a basket and a ball. It teaches teamwork, integrity respect. It is the ultimate game," said Bernert.

Val Ackerman, former president of the WNBA recalled the first game between the New York Liberty and Los Angeles Sparks on June 21, 1996: "The first game was as culmination of a great deal of effort and years of planning." For Ackerman it was a monumental day. She recalled noticing how nervous many of the players were. Many of them had been playing outside the United States for many years, so it was a homecoming for them to be back in this country playing basketball. "Ten years ago, no one expected that people would still be talking about the WNBA. We were determined to be the exception to all of those leagues that had come and gone," said Ackerman.

In her tenure with the WNBA and now with the national team, Ackerman has seen the game change dramatically. "We all predicted a revolutionary progression with the quality of play," said Ackerman. Younger players are redefining the game. Coaches, players, and fans of the game have undoubtedly noticed that players now are more athletic and more developed. Ackerman believes this progression is due in part to the WNBA not allowing early entry into the league: "Players attend college, gaining [not only] basketball knowledge, but social and personal growth. We've been very fortunate that our Player's Association has agreed to those minimum age requirements."

Ackerman agrees that there are business challenges as with any relatively new league, but women's basketball is marketable. She pointed to other professional leagues with their respective ups and downs. The NBA couldn't sell itself in the '60s and '70s. Tennis wasn't an easy sell in the '60s. Men's golf wasn't too successful until Tiger Woods came along. Ackerman is optimistic that the women's game will continue to grow.

Ackerman and many other agree that culturally, women's sports are up against different obstacles, but the passage of time will only help as the next generation of girls becomes women, as young boys grow up with young girls playing sports and become young fathers who think it's perfectly normal and natural for women to play sports and to pay money to watch them. "It may take a generation or two, but we are on that course. That first game June 21, 1996, is a moment in history for sure, for me just the beginning of something that will only get better with time," said Ackerman.

Doris Burke, television analyst, said of the WNBA, "It's a tremendous milestone to have reached ten years. They've achieved something that has not been achieved in the history of women's basketball in this country. The fact that the WNBA is on national television and is averaging 8,500 to 9,000 fans per game, that's cause for celebration." Burke has a daughter whose interests lie more in the theater and other sports, but as a parent, especially as a mother of a young daughter, the WNBA represents something to her beyond a professional sports league: "It shows me our society is making strides as to how it views women and that can only be good for every woman in any walk or way of life."

Hall of Famer and current analyst Nancy Lieberman said, "The WNBA has given women the chance on a major level to express themselves as to who and what they are and show their God-given skills. I appreciate that because we didn't have it when I was younger." Lieberman believes it is the role of former players and coaches to teach the younger players the history of the game. The younger players of today and tomorrow will one day become the history of the game. It's imperative for those who played the game and those who have been the gatekeepers of the game to make certain that the history of women's basketball is not lost on the younger generations.

Dan Hughes, head coach and general manager of the San Antonio Silver Stars, doesn't see a difference in coaching men and women. "If there is a difference, I feel like communication on a verbal scale is more versatile when coaching women versus coaching men. You can reach more female players by talking to them rather than by demonstrating or challenging their will, for example," he said. In his dual roles Hughes oversees the Silver Stars' basketball staff, the team's roster development, and all player acquisitions, all while also coaching the team.

Prior to joining the Silver Stars, Hughes spent a year serving as the Mid-American Conference (MAC) assistant commissioner for men's basketball operations and served as the head coach of the Cleveland Rockers from 2000 to 2003 before the team ceased operations in the fall of 2003.

Hughes was drawn to the women's game because of the opportunity and a general feeling that it was a great fit for him. He had been a Division I assistant coach, and there was an opportunity at the University of Toledo in the women's program. "My sister played as did many other relatives who were good women's players. I wish I could tell you it was some grand plan, but to be honest with you, the opportunity came to me. It just really fit," said Hughes. Hughes's first WNBA coaching assignment was the Charlotte Sting.

While serving as an assistant coach during the 1999 season, Hughes took over as head coach midway through the season, helping the Sting improve their standing in the Eastern Conference from fourth to second place. He led the team to its third consecutive playoff appearance and its first ever playoff series victory. In addition to his coaching responsibilities in Charlotte, Hughes was also a scout for the Charlotte Hornets during the WNBA's off-season.

During his four-year stint with the Rockers, Hughes posted a 66-64 record with three trips to the playoffs. In his first season in Cleveland, Hughes directed the team's resurgence from a 7-25 season in 1999 to a 17-15 finish in 2000 and was voted WNBA Coach of the Year runner-up. The following year Hughes was named 2001 WNBA Coach of the Year after leading the Rockers to a 22-10 record and to their second straight playoff appearance."

A native of Lowell, Ohio, Hughes has been involved in coaching basketball at almost every level. Prior to joining the Sting, he served as the assistant coach with the University of Toledo's women's basketball program (1996–97) and men's basketball program (1991–96). During his tenure with the Rockets' women's team, they posted a 27-4 record, winning the MAC Championship, and made an NCAA Tournament appearance. He also served as assistant coach with the men's teams at Mount Union College (1982–84) and (1985–91) and Baldwin-Wallace College (1984–85). During the 1977–78 season, Hughes was a graduate assistant at Miami of Ohio, helping the team to a MAC Championship and an appearance in the NCAA Regionals.[11]

Hughes noted that the combination of skill and athleticism has really grown since he began coaching women. Starting lineups in the WNBA are just so much more athletic, with so much more skill. "The league is so competitive that you can make strides with your team, but you're playing teams who have developed a really strong product," said Hughes.

The other factor Hughes cites in developing a WNBA team for a championship is the coaching of players who play all year, both in the WNBA and overseas. "So many athletes play virtually year-round, it's difficult to manage the preparation of players. There is a delicate balance between preparation and overuse," said Hughes. Because the WNBA season is so compressed, many players go overseas because they have the opportunity to make excellent money. "I never once tried to persuade a player to play or not play overseas. It's their decision. I do know this, when you get in your thirties and you're playing twelve months a year, that's a really difficult proposition for anyone," explained Hughes.

While the challenges remain, Hughes still loves to coach. Underneath it all, it's the teaching, it's the relating to players, the communication that sustains him or puts him in his "sweet spot" as Hughes likes to say. "As I get older, I think of myself less as a coach and more as a leader, just a leader of people, and in this case, of women," said Hughes. Helping an individual attain something within a group touches Hughes in way that is far more sustaining than how much money he makes. Don't let him kid you, he's still eyeing that WNBA championship trophy and the 2007 off season proved it. Hughes pulled off one of the biggest trades in WNBA history, trading first-round draft pick Jessica Davenport, their second overall selection in the 2007 WNBA draft, to the New York Liberty for Becky Hammon. Terms of the deal also give San Antonio New York's second-round 2008 selection, while New York will claim the lower selection between San Antonio and Detroit's 2008 first-round picks. While the news of the trade came as a surprise to Hammon, she was excited about playing for Hughes. "He really cares about his players on a personal level, and that means a great deal to me," she said.

Hughes is one of only nine other male coaches in the WNBA —a small number in comparison to other professional sports leagues. However, since there are only thirteen teams in the

WNBA, nine male head coaches is a high number. Only four women currently lead WNBA teams. They are Pat Coyle, New York Liberty; Anne Donovan, Seattle Storm; Jenny Boucek, Sacramento Monarchs; and Karleen Thompson, Houston Comets.

On one hand, as the talent pool increases in women's basketball, more parity will follow in the head coaching ranks. On the other hand, the argument can and should be made that coaches like Dan Hughes are a welcome addition to the WNBA, regardless of their sex. Hughes is a talented coach who believes in his players as people. For him, it makes no difference if his players are female or male. Basketball is basketball.

10 The Superstars and the "Special" Treatment

n 2005 I had the opportunity to speak with Connecticut's Nykesha Sales and Sacramento's Ticha Penicheiro. I met Nykesha Sales before the Connecticut Sun, New York Liberty matchup on August 20, 2005, at the Mohegan Sun Arena. As I entered the Sun locker room for the first time prior to a game, the only other player I saw was University of Connecticut standout Asjha Jones sitting in a large leather executive chair. Jones watched another WNBA game while she finished dressing as I sat with Sales.

Nykesha Sales is one of the most accomplished players in WNBA history. She's a smooth and versatile guard/forward who can shoot, rebound, pass, and defend. Her streak of 248 straight regular season starts, the second longest in WNBA history, ended on July 8, 2006, because of an Achilles tendon injury.

Sales spent her first four seasons in the league with the Orlando Magic, which was then moved to Connecticut under the Mohegan Sun's ownership. At UConn, she helped lead the Huskies to the 1995 NCAA Championship, a Final Four appearance in the 1996 NCAA Tournament, and Elite Eight appearances in 1997 and 1998.

Sales was guarded but relaxed when we spoke prior to a game on her home floor in the Mohegan Sun Arena. Clearly accustomed to the pregame activities of the press, she seemed to prefer going about the business of playing basketball, nothing more, nothing less.

Obviously the WNBA is a business, but Sales still enjoys getting out there and simply playing the game. "I enjoy trying to find ways to win. I enjoy the people around me. As an athlete, I enjoy competition. When it's not fun anymore, that's when it's time to retire, but I think all of us really enjoy what we do," said Sales.

Sales still doesn't take her abilities on the basketball court for granted. Smiling, she said, "I never, never, never take my abilities for granted because I realize how hard it is to stay in the league. Players really have to work in the off season. There are a lot of players who are really, really good in this league. I never take the opportunities I've had to play basketball for a living for granted. I don't take much for granted."

We continued to talk about the game. The longer we spoke, the more she relaxed she became. Although I had several more questions, I knew she was anxious to get out on the court. So I asked her one final question: What is your first memory with a basketball? She stopped for a moment and closed her eyes. I briefly scanned the locker room. Asjha Jones was gone. The locker room was empty except for the two of us. In that small, quiet moment, I felt as though I belonged. Before I let the feeling really sink in, I looked down at my feet and saw sandals instead of sneakers. Quickly like a candle blown out in a sharp wind, I was brought back to the singular reality that while basketball was my foundation, a WNBA locker room was not my home.

Sales answered my question slowly. "I remember learning how to shoot overhand. Because I started shooting the ball underhand, my cousin taught me how to shoot overhand. Ever since then it took off, and here I am," she said looking at the empty locker room.

Here we are, I thought.

The following week, I prepared for my interview with Ticha Penicheiro. This interview was handled differently because of her schedule and our locations. Ticha had a Sunday morning off, so we talked on the phone.

Ticha Penicheiro has played for the Sacramento Monarchs since being drafted in 1998 after graduating from Old Dominion. She was named an honorable mention to the WNBA's All-Decade Team, an honor saved for only fifteen players in WNBA history. Penicheiro is a four-time WNBA All-Star and is a member of the Portuguese national team. She represented her country for the first time when she was just fourteen years old. While at Old Dominion, Penicheiro was a Naismith Trophy finalist and winner of the Wade Trophy in 1998. She set an NCAA Final Four record with eight steals in the 1997 Championship Game loss to Tennessee.

Just as we began the interview, she excused herself so she could manage her black Labrador retriever. "He wants to play and is happy I'm home," she laughed. Once her dog was successfully restrained, we began our discussion talking about her experiences at Old Dominion. She said, "Old Dominion was huge for me as a woman and as a basketball player. I came from a different country and different culture. Without taking that step I wouldn't be in the WNBA right now."

We talked about a lot of things over the course of almost an hour, but I wanted to know about her love of the game. She said, "My love for the game is legit. It comes from my family. My dad and my brother passed it on to me. I still love it like I did when I was a child. It's not a struggle for me. I don't do it for the money. I do it because I have a lot of fun. It comes from my heart." Penicheiro, like so many other players, credits her family. For her family and basketball are her top priorities in life. "I take a lot of pride in what I do. Every day I wake up and feel blessed," she said.

Sometimes Penicheiro reads fan letters from kids who can't

play basketball because they are sick. That's a constant reminder for her to count her blessings every day. She said, "I am in a position I never thought I'd be in. I've worked hard all my life, I've been blessed with great family support, and without that, I probably wouldn't be here today. It's important that you count your blessings every day because you don't know when that can be taken away from you."

Ticha's first memory with a basketball is still strong. Her dad and brother passed on the love of the game to her, although the early rejections she felt on the playground are still vivid: "Usually, I was the only girl playing with all the boys. I was rejected a lot early on. I was skinny and I was a girl, so the boys didn't want me to play because they thought I'd get hurt."

The process of acceptance for Penicheiro was not easy. Like every other kid on the playground, she had to prove herself and also prove that girls can play as well as the boys can. She said, "Slowly I started to get accepted, and I continued to work hard. I dribbled the ball to school, dribbled it home. I always had a basketball in my hands." Penicheiro and so many players at all levels recall those early moments with a basketball like it was yesterday. The conversations between their bodies and the ball, between their teammates and adversaries leave indelible marks on the kinds of players they will ultimately become.

The Veterans

Basketball is ultimately about communication. It is one of the most truthful and honest ways we communicate. It's a conduit for an adrenaline rush—the anticipation of a battle and the potential satisfaction of coming out victorious. Off the court we camouflage our true selves. We wear masks, but on the court, truth reigns. You can't hide on a court. You can't pretend to be courageous. You can't pretend to be smart. You have to prove it. If you can't prove it, you sit next to the coach on the sideline and hope for another chance.

Moreover, the kind of player you are probably mirrors the kind of person you are. Are you a ball hog? Will you ignore an open teammate just to hit your scoring average? Do you lead your team or become invisible when the score is tied with two seconds left? Some players are quiet. Role players fill this category. They don't talk trash, and they don't celebrate. Day in and day out, they come to play. Hard. They're the ones who set the killer screens and box out each and every shot. They come to do the dirty work that wins games with little or no congratulations. There are others who are vocal leaders. They want the ball in their hands when all looks lost. Players like Diana Taurasi, Tamika Catchings, Sheryl Swoopes, and Lisa Leslie epitomize these players. They want the pressure of winning or losing on their heads. They'll accept full responsibility if the shot is missed and will give credit to their teammates if the shot is made, but these players have a compulsion to be in the game in order to take on that responsibility.

Vickie Johnson currently plays for the San Antonio Silver Stars, although she spent most of her career with the New York Liberty. Johnson is only one of three players in WNBA history to have scored more than 3,000 career points, grabbed 1,000 rebounds, and dished out more than 750 assists. She is one of only five players in the league to have played every season and is a two-time WNBA All-Star (1999, 2001).

Dan Hughes, Johnson's current head coach in San Antonio, couldn't say enough about her. He said, "V.J. has brought a maturity to our team about how to be a professional, and she has done it in the most effective way—peer to peer. She knows where we're going, but she can relate it in player's terms to younger players in moments I can't as a coach. V.J. is an example of what every veteran should be. The fans here in San Antonio love her, but I don't know if nationally fans appreciate all that she's done for the WNBA. I wish they would. V.J. is a joy to coach. She is every reason why I want to coach. She is a pure pleasure."

Johnson's current longtime teammate, Becky Hammon, said that Johnson is one of the most competitive people she has ever played with. Hammon recalled her first years in the WNBA with the New York Liberty, learning from veterans like Johnson and Teresa Weatherspoon. She said, "The veterans on that New York team never sat out a practice. You'll get a lot of big superstars who get an ache or a pain, and they sit out of practice. Those two would go hard at each other. They loved competing. That's something I learned from V.J.—we could go really hard at each other in practice then walk off the court and be totally cool. V.J. is truly someone who doesn't talk a lot, but what she says she means, and you can take it to the bank."

Johnson talked about her years in a New York Liberty uniform. She said, "I love New York, I've always loved New York. My heart and soul is in New York, but life is about changes. I asked God to lead me to the right place, and San Antonio was the place for me."

Johnson also commented on Dan Hughes and his abilities as a coach. She said of Hughes, "He really cares about you, about how you are doing, how your family is doing. He understands that we are more than just athletes. He doesn't care if you're the starter or a rookie, he's going to respect you as a player and as a person."

Johnson has remained motivated in the WNBA by taking each day as a new challenge. She loves the competition and wants only to play against the best basketball players in the world. She strives to improve her game because she doesn't believe that she has played the best basketball of her career yet. "I refuse to play only for the money. I play because I love the game and I love to compete. When that changes, then I'll retire."

Johnson recalls playing basketball for the first time when she was nine years old. She has three brothers and cousins who were always playing hoops. "I remember the first time I played, my brother said, 'I don't want you to get hurt. Basketball is not for girls, it's for guys only. Girls can't play this game because it is too physical.' That was my motivation."

For Johnson basketball mimics life. There is an action and a reaction—offense and defense. "As a person you must adjust to the challenges you face in life. Basketball is about changes and sacrifices. It's about making the right decisions at the right time. I play for the challenge of competing and what I can do to prove to myself and to other people. I play for the unity of the team. Everyone has to put her personal ego aside in order to come together to win a championship," she said.

Crystal Robinson, Johnson's former longtime teammate in New York, agreed. Robinson retired from the Washington

Mystics in June of 2007 but continued on as an assistant coach for the team. She said, "Making it to the WNBA Finals with my New York Liberty team was really special because we had such great chemistry in New York." Crystal Robinson was Vickie Johnson's teammate for eight seasons until both were traded prior to the 2006 season. Prior to entering the WNBA, Robinson played for Southeast Oklahoma State.

Robinson knew she was good enough to compete at a higher level when she started playing USA Basketball in the Olympic Festival out of high school. While she played AAU in high school, the Olympic Festival provided the opportunity to play against other All-Stars and talented athletes. Over the years Robinson's love for the sport has not diminished. "I love that basketball is a team sport. I love the camaraderie. No other kind of job has the atmosphere that lets you develop this kind of camaraderie with your teammates. You live together, you get to know your teammates, and you go through struggles with other people. You learn to accept people's differences and work with them. The game teaches you such great life lessons because you have been a part of a team and you know what it takes to fight through everyone's differences, to all have one common goal."

Like Johnson Robinson just loves the game. She said, "Everyone wants to be the best. Everyone wants to get that ring. Everybody wants to go down in history as someone who has really accomplished something." To some players in the league, the game becomes a job, but players like Johnson, Robinson, Sales, and Penicheiro play it because they simply love competing at the highest level possible. For those players and coaches who are lucky enough to play and coach professionally, it just so happens that they finally found some people in the United States who pay them to do it.

Economy Class

After hitting the eleven-year mark, the WNBA still does pay its players, albeit a ridiculously low salary in comparison to their male counterparts in the NBA. The players and the WNBA management understand the challenges of growing their collective market share. They all know that when they can translate all those statistics of interested fans of women's sports into actual ticket and merchandising sales, advertising and television contracts will follow. Only then will salaries increase.

In the meantime the players in the WNBA continue to fly economy class. They handle their own baggage and grab quick meals like the rest of us at the fast-food kiosks in airports around the country. In comparison, the players in the NBA fly in chartered private jets. They don't struggle through airport security lines or sit cramped in coach seats. Very often their meals are carefully planned and provided for them. The NBA's Miami Heat owned a private Boeing jet, which was highlighted on a recent Discovery Channel program. A segment of the program was dedicated to showing off the jet and how the NBA players travel. In a nutshell the players have ample legroom for their long frames. The regular staff knows what candy or snack each player enjoys while flying and stock that candy next to the individual player's private seat. The media that cover the Miami Heat on a regular basis also travel on the private jet with the team. There's a separate section for the coaching staff so they can go over scouting reports or discuss game plans without bothering the players. One of the Miami Heat players who narrated this segment beamed proudly as he showed off the Boeing jet. He was particularly proud of the Miami Heat logo on the fin of the plane.

It couldn't be more different for the women in the WNBA. Not once have I seen a WNBA player pleased to be traveling or pleased to show off her accommodations. In 2005 when I followed the New York Liberty through their season, I traveled on most of their flights, with a birds-eye view of the players' behavior and interactions with other travelers. I watched in horror as they bought Big Macs and fast food on game days. They dressed casually and stayed in small groups of two or three in the airport gate waiting areas. Once or twice I saw another traveler eye the players and ask if they were athletes. For the most part the Liberty players came and went virtually unrecognized through airport after airport. Once seated on the plane, the players spoke little and just tried to sleep or read their way through the flights. If you weren't conscious of their presence, you'd never notice them.

Some WNBA organizations already own private jets, but the league won't allow those teams to use their jets to shuttle WNBA teams because they believe it would be an unfair advantage. In other words, teams that travel well play better than teams that travel like baggage. If a WNBA team uses a private jet, they're slapped with a hefty fine.

While the players do stay at very nice hotels, they spend so little time in the hotel it doesn't really matter. This is the magical life of a WNBA player. While they might customarily play in front of crowds of six to ten thousand fans a night, their lives are not the lives of superstars. They move through public spaces quietly. They travel from game to game at a dizzying speed throughout the hot summer months without complaint or even much money to show for it. If you ask any of them, they will continue to do it because it means playing in the United States. Collectively the players will sacrifice in order to ensure the league's longevity.

Different but Not Worse Than

Many basketball fans complain that the women's game isn't as entertaining to watch as the men's game. Analyst Doris Burke is surprised at the negativity. Burke acknowledges that an important demographic watching sports today is the eighteen- to thirty-five-year-old male. "In the first two years of the league, that demographic didn't give the WNBA a second look. I don't think people's perceptions have kept pace with the increased quality of play in the WNBA today. The level of basketball is finally at a place where it's enjoyable to watch."

Why is it so difficult for people to understand that the women's game is different from the men's, different but not worse than? The women's game is changing, and it's changing fast. When was the last time you heard of an NBA rookie earning thirty-one thousand dollars a year and being thrilled by the opportunity to play basketball at the highest level? When was the last time you heard of an NBA veteran traveling coach across the country for back-to-back games and not complaining about how hard his life is?

Some sports fans might recall Philadelphia Eagle wide receiver

Terrell Owens suspended in 2005 for remarking that his team should have thrown a ticker-tape parade in honor of his one-hundredth reception. When was the last time you heard a female athlete make that kind of claim?

Forget about the salary difference. The minimum salary for an NBA rookie is $412,718. For veterans that number jumps to over $17 million a year. In the WNBA a rookie can't earn less than $32,400, as set by the league. A WNBA veteran can't earn more than $93,000. The WNBA's entire team salary cap of $728,000 doesn't even come close to paying for two NBA rookies. While the NBA players are rolling in the money and traveling in deluxe accommodations, they are able to focus their energies on their job, playing basketball.

The key is the women of the WNBA don't complain; although if they did, they'd certainly be branded as crybabies and whiners. Many players I spoke to said they wished they lived like their counterparts in the NBA, but they loved the game. One player who wished to remain anonymous told me, "Life for women in the WNBA is no picnic during the summer months. We earn little money for our hard work. But we love what we do, and we want to support a professional league in the United States."

The WNBA can market inspiration all they want, and they should. There are plenty of inspirational stories. Perhaps they can start by acknowledging that while the WNBA is a business, it's never been about the money for the players. If it were only about the money, none of them would be in the United States. They'd be overseas, making far more money per minute on the floor.

Part five USA Basketball

11 The United States versus the Rest of the World

The Olympic Games are part of the fabric of our American sports culture. Shirl J. Hoffman, in his book titled *Sport as Religion*, states that "sport has long been regarded as a shaper and a reinforcer of values deemed critical to the maintenance of American society."[1] Perhaps one need not look further than the Olympic Games for a better, more potent example of values like hard work, dedication, teamwork, and perseverance than USA Basketball and the Women's National Team.

While many avidly follow the Americans' successes and failures during the Olympic Games, the games themselves are the culmination of years of hard work and planning by thousands of individuals. The organization that oversees Olympic basketball in the United States is USA Basketball. "USA Basketball is a nonprofit organization and the national governing body for men's and women's basketball in the United States, headquartered in Colorado Springs, Colorado. As the recognized governing body for basketball in the United States by the International Basketball Federation (FIBA) and the United States Olympic Committee (USOC), USA Basketball is responsible for the selection; training and fielding of USA teams that compete in FIBA sponsored international basketball competitions, as well as for some national competitions."[2] If you're interested in understanding exactly how USA Basketball is structured, check out appendix B.

The Long and Winding Road

As girls' basketball grows in participation and interest around the country, so does interest in the Women's National Team. Carol Callan, executive director of women's programs at USA Basketball, said, "We are extremely lucky in this country because we have large numbers of girls playing this game and we have a strong development system through the school-based organizations."

For those young athletes interested in one day being a part of the Women's National Team, the road is long and extremely competitive. The progression for most young kids is to begin playing in a youth-league environment. From there they move onto school teams. In high school the more interested players supplement their school-team experience with AAU and various summer leagues.

The first real step for talented basketball players is to receive an invitation to the Youth Development Festival. A committee composed of high school and AAU representatives chooses thirty-six to forty-eight high-school juniors. These representatives utilize their personal networks to determine who knows who the top players in their regions are. This list is then supplemented by feedback from thirty colleges and universities across the country. This process helps ensure that no one person has too much weight on the committee. Carol Callan said, "We want to be inclusive. We want to do a good job. Some people believe our process to be political, but having been a part of it from all angles, it's really as unpolitical a process as it can be."

Clay Kallam from *Full Court Press* recently commented on the Youth Development Festival. He wrote, "Evaluating talent is always tricky, but one of the proclaimed values of summer basketball is that it gives everyone—players, coaches and parents—a chance to see the best go against the best."[3]

Once an athlete becomes involved in the USA Basketball program, the organization then wants to develop those athletes for the international scene. Because the international game is so different and because the level of competition is so high, it's vital for the young athletes to work through the USA Basketball program step by step. Carol Callan said, "Dawn Staley and Lisa Leslie are two great examples. They started in 1989 and virtually have played every year since. That's the way you win. We want to develop players and track them as they go through our system."

Should a player not participate in the Under 18 (U18) team or the Youth Development Festival, there are still avenues and opportunities to get on the radar. A collegiate committee selects players the top thirty to thirty-five athletes regionally to participate in either the Under 21 (U21) FIBA World Championships or the World University Games. Obviously at the senior level, there should be no surprises. "Our philosophy is we invest a tremendous amount in players who have worked through our system. We train them in the international game. Because so many of our WNBA athletes play overseas, they know the international game well," said Callan.

The Masterminds

Denise Lardner Carmody wrote in her article titled "Big-Time Spectator Sports," musing on the stereotype of female athletes, "Men in our culture have been raised to compete while women have been raised to cooperate."[4] The success of the Senior Women's National Basketball Team in the 1996 Olympic Games wasn't just a celebration of female competition. The insiders who made the Olympic success possible also gave new meaning to cooperation and dogged determination. "The 1996 Olympic Games in Atlanta was just a wonderful experience. I burst into tears when we won the gold medal. It was a very emotional day," said Val Ackerman, current president of USA Basketball and former president of the WNBA.

The success of the 1996 Senior Women's National Team was the culmination of a great deal of effort, and that effort was expended by more than just the players on the court. There was a great deal of convincing to be done as Val Ackerman recalled: "We needed to convince people that the team must be together for a full year, that we could find a way to pay for it, that we could get a coach who would take a year off from her program to coach it. Nobody believed that would happen."

The 1996 team was modeled in many ways on the men's Dream Team. Program insiders wanted to bring together the top players and prepare them for the Atlanta Games. However, they also believed that if the country could see women's basketball at the highest level, they would become more interested in the women's game and more supportive of the Senior Women's National Team.

ABC and ESPN signed on for a ten-game television package. Sponsors signed on. The cover of the *Sports Illustrated* 1996 Olympic preview showcased the Women's Senior National Team with Teresa Edwards, Katrina McClain, Rebecca Lobo, Lisa Leslie, and Dawn Staley. Ackerman said, "Seeing that magazine cover was an incredible moment. NBA commissioner David Stern and I were headed into a meeting with ESPN to discuss their TV deal for the WNBA, and we were able to bring that cover to the meeting."

Ackerman was the founding president of the Women's National Basketball Association and was elected president of USA Basketball in March 2005. Ackerman is the first female president of USA Basketball and has been associated with USA Basketball since 1990. She served on the USA Basketball board of directors for the 1990–92, 1992–96, and 2000–2004 terms and on the organization's executive committee as secretary from 1996 to 2000. She was a driving force behind the creation of the historic 1995–96 USA Basketball Women's Senior National Team program that culminated with a 60-0 record and the gold medal at the 1996 Atlanta Olympics.

Ackerman framed the success in the 1996 Olympics in terms

of women's sports in the '90s. She pointed to UConn's undefeated season in 1995 because that team's success mobilized writers in the Northeast who until that time had not been paying attention to what was going on in women's basketball. That fall, the national team was assembled. Ackerman said, "The period from 1994 to 2000 was an incredible time for women's sports, ultimately taking women's team sports to a completely new level.

Carol Callan was also instrumental in bringing the 1996 team together. She said, "For that gold medal game, there was no way we were going to lose. I can remember hugging people after the game ended. It was a release of pure joy. It was an indescribable feeling."

After overseeing all facets of the historic 1995–96 USA Basketball Women's National Team and assisting with the 1996 U.S. Olympic Women's Basketball Team, Carol Callan assumed duties as assistant executive director for women's programs in October 1996. Callan is responsible for all USA Basketball women's team programs, including competitions, trials, and training camps and serves as a liaison to women's competition committees. Callan's job is to ensure that the coaches can coach and the players can play, and play successfully: "I'm biased, but I don't think there is anything better than what I get to watch on a daily basis. I work with the people who are the very best at what they do. I get great satisfaction watching it all come together, and I get great satisfaction out of watching us win."

A driving force behind the historic first-time national team program, Callan was responsible for team logistics, travel, and scheduling of games and training. "Prior to taking the reins of the national team program, Callan was involved with USA Basketball for almost seven years as a volunteer committee member. She served on USA Basketball's Executive Committee as secretary from 1992 to 1995. From 1989 to 1995 she was a member of the Women's Player Selection Committee and served as chair from 1992–1995. Additionally, Callan was a member of the Women's Programs Committee from 1992 to 1995."[5]

Although the Senior Women's National Team did not win the gold medal at the recent World Championships in Brazil (they captured the bronze), Ackerman and Callan remain optimistic about the future of the team, specifically the 2008 Olympics in Beijing. Both are convinced that continuity is the primary buzzword for the national team program. Keeping players together is a difficult task because of the WNBA and overseas seasons.

Scheduling aside Ackerman and Callan both agree that USA Basketball is in good hands. "We couldn't script the passing of the torch in Women's National Team basketball any better," said Ackerman. From Katrina McClain and Teresa Edwards to Dawn Staley, Lisa Leslie, and Sheryl Swoopes, commitment in the program remained steadfast. Superstars like Sue Bird, Diana Taurasi, Tamika Catchings, and Candace Parker are now taking the reins.

Both Callan and Ackerman are responsible for amazing strides in the women's game, and both are quick to credit the level of pride by the athletes and coaches involved. "It's really a fascinating distinction between the men and the women. On the women's side, we've been very fortunate that the top women's players want to play for the national team, event in and event out. There really is no stopping them. Teresa Edwards participated in five Olympic Games, and if the rest of them are healthy and able, they would do it if they could," said Ackerman.

It is evident that the best women's players recognize participation in the Senior National Team as an incredible honor, and they remain committed to the program's success. Ackerman and Callan believe that commitment has made the program successful because it ensures continuity in the program. Callan said, "Some players play for the fame and the glory. Some players play for the purity of the game. To be a part of the Olympic experience, a player must become more than just an elite athlete. Not everyone can be an Olympian." Callan believes that the athletes who have participated in multiple Olympic Games have more than talent.

Clearly the women who participate in the Olympics really enjoy being a part of it and representing the United States. Winning championships is never easy. As the world gets better, it will be more difficult, but these women are resilient and are committed to continuing their reign.

12 The Best in the World

Coaching the most talented female basketball players in the world cannot be an easy task. It takes a special personality. It takes tremendous skill. It takes years of experience. It also doesn't hurt to have been an Olympic gold medalist too.

Basketball gave Anne Donovan an identity outside of her family, and for that she is grateful. "I was a very quiet and withdrawn kid growing up and came from a very close-knit family. Basketball was a great fit for me, a natural fit, not just because of my height, just because it felt so comfortable and became such a passion for me," said Donovan, currently the head coach of the Women's Senior National Team in addition to her duties as head coach of the WNBA's Seattle Storm.

Donovan's first time representing the United States of America came in 1978 at the early age of fifteen. Throughout the history of Olympic and World Championship play, only two other U.S. athletes, Pat Summitt and Alberta Cox, have returned as an Olympic or World Championship head coach. Commitment and dedication to the Olympic program have remained in Donovan's blood. Most of her life has been built around USA Basketball in some capacity, and she's quick to articulate her pride in the program: "The opportunity to both play and coach in the Olympic program is not taken for granted by me. With it comes great responsibility to carry on the tradition, and it's something I take great pride in."

In addition to her three Olympic teams (1980, DNC; 1984, gold; 1988, gold) as an athlete, Donovan served as assistant coach to Van Chancellor (Houston Comets) in 2004 as the United States earned the gold medal in Athens. Donovan was an assistant coach for the 1998 and 2002 gold-medal-winning FIBA World Championship squads. She played on the 1986 USA World Championship Team that took down the USSR by a score of 108–88 in Moscow for the gold medal and the 1983 USA World Championship Team that captured the silver medal after losing 84–82 in a battle with the Soviet Union in the gold medal game. Donovan returned from the 2004 Games leading the Seattle Storm to the WNBA crown. In doing so Donovan became the first female coach to head a WNBA championship team.

Donovan has been involved in the USA Basketball organization since 1978 as a player, coach, and committee member. Her 2006 World Championship appointment marks Donovan's fifth coaching assignment with USA Basketball and first as a head coach. She has adapted through the years, as the levels have changed, but her core principals remain the same: "I love the fundamentals of the game. For me success is predicated on those fundamentals."

Adhering to those fundamentals has served Donovan well.

In addition to acting as an assistant to Chancellor at the 2004 Olympics, where the team went unscathed through competition at 8-0, and the 2002 World Championship, where the USA finished with a perfect 9-0 mark, Donovan was also on the sidelines both of those years as the USA Basketball Women's Senior National Team posted a 16-0 record in exhibition play prior to Athens and in 2002 the U.S. earned the Australian-hosted 2002 Opals World Challenge title with a 4-0 record. In 1998, Donovan served as an assistant coach to Nell Fortner with the USA World Championship Team that captured the gold medal in Germany. Donovan assisted Fortner and the 1997 USA Women's World Championship Qualifying Team that went 4-2, earned the silver medal in Brazil and qualified the U.S. for the '98 Worlds.

In all, USA Basketball teams with Donovan on the sidelines have racked up an impressive 75-4 record for a sterling 94.9 winning percentage and she brings with her into 2006 a USA Basketball 54 game-winning streak, dating to April 28, 1998.[1]

Carol Callan commented on Donovan's success with USA Basketball: "Anne is such an ambassador for women's coaches and the women's game. She has shown she knows how to win." Val Ackerman made it clear that Donovan was the natural candidate to be the head coach. Donovan earned the opportunity. "There was really no second choice. She is an Olympian, a highly successful WNBA coach, a national team assistant, she has everything we need," said Ackerman.

Inducted as a player into the Naismith Basketball Hall of Fame in 1995 and into the Women's Basketball Hall of Fame in 1999, Donovan has been a player on a remarkable eleven USA Basketball teams and is one of the most decorated players in USA Basketball history. She played on the 1980, 1984, and 1988 Olympic teams and the 1983 and 1986 World Championship teams. All told, of a possible ten medals she has captured seven golds and two silvers as a player and posted a 52-7 record for an astounding 88.1 winning percentage.

As a player and coach Donovan has seen the international women's game change significantly over the years. Although the WNBA game is physical, Donovan notes that the international game is a different kind of physical. The physicality in the paint is at a different level than in the WNBA. The contact on the ball handler is different. From a technical standpoint, the rules are also slightly different than in the WNBA.

Donovan has also seen firsthand how much international competition has changed over last two decades. The United States spent years trying to catch the Soviets, but in the mid-1980s, the shift was on. From there, the United States has held the gold-medal position for the better part of the last two decades. Over the years the rest of the world has fervently worked to catch up to the United States. "Everyone else has studied us and worked hard to topple us, and the rest of the world has come pretty darned close in the last eight years," explained Donovan.

She also believes that the WNBA provides other countries an opportunity to closely study the U.S. style of play. "International players enter the WNBA, they study how we play the game, what our strengths are, how we utilize our strengths," said Donovan. In addition U.S. players head overseas to play when the WNBA season concludes, so U.S. athletes are no longer an unknown commodity. They are thoroughly scouted by the outside coaching world and the players.

Donovan took over the reins of the Seattle Storm in 2003 and led them to an 18-16 record, the most victories in franchise history. In the next two seasons Donovan not only increased the Storm's overall record to 20-14 in each of those two years, she also piloted her 2004 team to their first ever WNBA title. Regarding her experiences in Seattle, Donovan explained, "There is no comparison to the energy in our building and our fans. Probably every coach in the WNBA will say that about his or her fans, but I say it sincerely. It's one of the best environments in the WNBA. We have a unique and special situation." On August 18, 2005, Donovan became the fourth WNBA coach, and first woman, to reach the one-hundred-victory milestone in a contest against the Minnesota Lynx.

Prior to joining the professional coaching ranks, Donovan spent three seasons (1995–96 to 1997–98) as head mentor at East Carolina University in North Carolina.

Donovan's motivation is simple—winning—although she's quick to point out that basketball is not only about winning. "The reason why I'm in basketball is no secret: it's people, it's relationships, it's just a great opportunity to connect with people about something I'm passionate about," said Donovan. One of the most accomplished players in collegiate women's basketball, Donovan helped guide Old Dominion University (ODU) to a sterling 37-1 record in 1980 as a freshman. She went on to lead ODU to the NCAA Final Four in 1983. With Donovan wearing the Old Dominion uniform, ODU compiled a remarkable 116-20 record (.853). She was named the Naismith and Champion Player of the Year in 1983 as well as an All-American in 1981, 1982, and 1983. Donovan finished her playing career at Old Dominion as the Lady Monarchs' all-time leading scorer (2,719), rebounder (1,976), and shot blocker (801) and still owns no less than twenty-five ODU records.

On October 24, 2004, the Sun Belt Conference named Donovan as its All-Time Women's Basketball Player. Additionally Donovan is a member of the Virginia Sports Hall of Fame, ODU Sports Hall of Fame, and the COSIDA Academic All-American Hall of Fame. After college Donovan spent five seasons playing professionally in Shizuoka, Japan (1983–84 to 1987–88), and one season in Modena, Italy (1988–89), before returning to Old Dominion as an assistant coach for six seasons (1989–90 to 1994–95). Donovan concluded, "I've been a part of the Olympic Games in Athens and the world championship with the Seattle Storm in 2004, and both coaching memories for me are prominent." As a player Donovan points to winning gold medals in Los Angeles and Seoul, Korea: "Seoul was extremely meaningful. It was the only Olympic experience I had in the three times I competed where the Games were not affected by any boycott."

Donovan conveys a quiet confidence about the game. She is serious about it and serious about winning. When Donovan talks, she sounds like an Olympian. She sounds as though she's been into battle and come out the other side. Those experiences only make her a better coach to other Olympians and to her WNBA team.

The Future Olympians

As a WNBA and Women's Senior National Team head coach, Donovan has the opportunity to work with the best and brightest playing talents in the world. Recently Donovan talked about Diana Taurasi, superstar from UConn, currently playing for both the Phoenix Mercury and the USA Women's Senior National Team. Donovan said of Taurasi, "I have to say, her passion is contagious. It's a passion for life, period. Diana just has a good time. One of her biggest thrills is the game of basketball. To be around her when she is enjoying that is a pleasure for all of us."

The mark of a stellar player is making the players around her better. To Donovan Taurasi exhibits that quality and then some. From a mental standpoint, Donovan believes that the confidence Taurasi gives her teammates is superb. "Taurasi's work ethic makes her the player she is. She sticks around after practice to shoot the ball another one to two hundred times. She is one of the most special players in this game, and she will lead the way when we go to Beijing," said Donovan.

Taurasi was the youngest member of the 2004 United States Women's Basketball Gold Medal Olympic Team in Athens, Greece. She earned a bronze medal as a member of the 2001 USA Junior World Championship team, earned a gold medal as a member of the 2000 USA Basketball Women's Junior World Championship Qualifying team, and was a member of the 2001 All-Fiba Junior World Championship team. Taurasi led UConn to three consecutive national championships under head coach Geno Auriemma. She won the 2003 and 2004 Naismith Player of the Year Awards as the best female player in the nation and was the first player in UConn history to finish career with 2,000 points, 600 assists, and 600 rebounds. In the WNBA Taurasi became only the second player in Phoenix Mercury franchise history to score over 1,000 points in her first two seasons. She's also become a regular fixture at the annual WNBA All-Star Game.

Thus far Taurasi's experience with the USA Senior Women's National Team has been positive because of the transition from veteran leadership to younger players. She said, "We've had great leaders in the past like Lisa Leslie, Sheryl Swoopes, Dawn Staley, and so on. Those players were committed to USA Basketball for many years. That's something for the younger players to emulate." That veteran leadership in USA Basketball is one of the main reasons why Taurasi feels she's successful at the international level. The professionalism of the veterans and their love of the national team experience haven't been lost on Taurasi.

International game or WNBA game, pickup game or practice, Taurasi just loves to play. "It's my life. I take pride in how hard I play and work. In basketball and in life, if you sell yourself short, you'll look back and be disappointed that you didn't take advantage of opportunities," said Taurasi.

One of Taurasi's teammates on the Senior Women's National Team is Tamika Catchings. Catchings regularly tops the list in vote getting for the WNBA All-Star Game and is a customary candidate for WNBA MVP and Defensive Player of the Year honors. She's led her Indiana Fever in points, rebounds, assists, and steals in each of her seasons. She was named the Defensive Player of the Year in 2005 and was third in balloting for MVP. She is the fastest in WNBA history to reach each of four significant milestones: 2,000 points, 1,000 rebounds, 400 assists, and 300 steals.

Doris Burke, a television analyst, admitted that watching Catchings perform night in and night out is a pleasure for her: "Number one, she's highly skilled. You have to check her for a lot of different things. She can shoot from the perimeter, she can post it up, she can take you off the bounce, and she can rebound with the best of them." Couple those skills with this relentless work ethic, and it's no surprise why Catchings has become WNBA royalty. "There may be more talented players, but I don't know how many of players play harder than she does with that collection of abilities," said Burke.

With regard to USA Basketball, Catchings admitted always wanting to be a part of the program. She points to the success of the 1996 Senior Women's National Team as a turning point for her. Although she had already played on some junior teams with USA Basketball, she recalls watching that team perform and finally understanding what USA Basketball was all about: "I just remember watching those ladies, knowing that they represented our country. I wanted to be there. I wanted to be one of them." According to Catchings, all of her experiences with USA Basketball have been wonderful, but to finally get the opportunity to play with Sheryl Swoopes, Lisa Leslie, and Dawn Staley was extremely special for her: "I remember just looking up to them. I wanted to be at the level that they were at. They really know what it takes to win a gold medal."

Catchings looks forward to the future of USA Basketball. She knows her generation is charged with taking the program to the next level, and she understands how important it is for every player involved in USA Basketball to be a team player. "We learned how to put our egos aside in order to be successful. That's what USA Basketball is all about. It's not about you, it's not about whatever WNBA team you play for, it's about the USA—how we represent our home country, how we win a gold medal. That's what's important. I take pride in representing our country because not many players get the chance," said Catchings.

Dawn Staley, USA Senior National Team assistant coach said of Taurasi and Catchings, "They're young, they're our future. They both have played on different USA Basketball teams, and they understand what goes into it. They can now lend their experiences to younger players coming up. That's the cycle that USA Basketball breeds."

Not Her Second Nature, Her First

Dawn Staley is women's basketball royalty. She came from the projects of Philadelphia, playing at Dobbins Tech High School from 1986 to 1989, leading her team to three straight Philadelphia Public League championships. People began to take notice when she was named *USA Today*'s National High School Player of the Year.

Staley played her college ball at the University of Virginia (UVA) (1989–92). She was a three-time Kodak All-American, leading UVA to a 110-21 record and four appearances in the NCAA Tournament. Three of those trips led to Final Four appearances. In 1991 the Cavaliers were the national runners-up. She is ranked sixth all-time on the NCAA's career steals list with 454 and was named the National Player of the Year in 1991 and 1992. In addition she was the ACC Conference Player of the Year in 1991 and 1992 and the Rookie of the Year in 1989. She is the only player, male or female, in ACC history to tally more than two thousand points, seven hundred rebounds, seven hundred assists, and four hundred steals and was just the second person in conference history to record a triple-double, a feat she did twice. To commemorate twenty-five years of Division I basketball, ESPN.com voted Staley one of the Top Players of the Past Twenty-Five Years.

From 1992 to 1994 Staley played professional basketball overseas in France, Italy, Brazil, and Spain. In 1994 she returned to American soil and competed for USA Basketball in the Goodwill Games and the World Championships. That year, Staley was named USA Basketball Female Athlete of the Year. In 1996 Staley guided the historic USA Basketball Women's team that captured the gold medal at the Olympic Games in Atlanta.

Staley didn't begin her United States professional playing career in the WNBA because the WNBA was not yet in existence. Therefore, she joined the Richmond Rage of the American Basketball League (ABL) in 1996–97 and helped the team to the ABL finals in addition to being named a two-time ABL All-Star. Staley then moved to the WNBA as the number-nine pick of the Charlotte Sting in the 1999 WNBA draft. In the summer of 2005 Staley was traded to the Houston Comets.

During the summer of 2000, Staley was named a member of the first women's Dream Team, a collection of women's professional players that represented the United States in the Olympic Games in Sydney, Australia. In the summer of 2004 she captured her third Olympic gold medal, leading Team USA to a perfect 8-0 record in the 2004 Games in Athens, Greece. She was selected by the other Olympic athletes to be the United States flag bearer for the opening ceremonies.

Although Staley retired from Olympic competition after the 2004 Games, she continues to be involved with USA Basketball. She was elected by a vote of USA Basketball's current athletes as an athlete representative on the USA Basketball executive committee in May of 2005. In February of 2006 Staley was selected as an assistant coach for the 2006 USA Women's World Championship Team. For Staley USA Basketball represents a purity of the game: "You know why you are there, you know that it's very different from any other team you have played on. You know that you must sacrifice for the good of the team. That sacrifice allows the team to come together for one common goal, and that goal is to win a gold medal."

Staley recognizes that in the WNBA if a player is a superstar on her team, she is expected to take all the big shots, and the offense is most likely developed around her. Staley explains that USA Basketball strips players of that ego in order to build them up within the system: "You can appreciate being there, you can appreciate when you are able to play a lot of minutes, and you can cherish that time."

Staley's transition from playing USA Basketball to becoming an assistant coach for the Senior Women's National Team wasn't too difficult. "My approach is the same. My job is to prepare players for their moment," said Staley.

Staley admits that the competitive mindset of USA Basketball is intense. "When we play, we try to destroy every team we face. Our opponents don't approach it that way. They're just jockeying for position to not play us in the medal round. We give it our all every time we step out on the floor. I wouldn't change that one bit."

Dawn Staley retired from WNBA competition following the 2006 season but not before leaving quite a legacy. During the 2006 season, she was voted an All-Star for the fifth time, becoming the first player in WNBA history to play for both the East and the West squads. Staley was also honored as a member of the WNBA's All-Decade team.

Staley has definitely noticed changes in the new players entering the WNBA ranks. She said, "I think with the young players, I'm seeing a different movement. They're young, they are talented, they are gifted, strong, athletic, smart. They've had the WNBA to aspire to for over ten years." While Staley admits that the WNBA is a fantastic outlet for talented players, she is quick to point out that with talent comes responsibility. She wants the younger players to understand the history of the women's game and where it must go moving forward: "It just doesn't stop with their contribution on the floor. It means also working to ensure that our league stays around forever. The young players don't know. They have not gone without the league. They don't understand what it means to have no options in the United States."

Staley fears that some of the younger players take the WNBA for granted because they just don't know any different. She said, "They've really haven't been taught. They've watched. We all did whatever it took to ensure that if female professional players don't want to go overseas to play, they don't have to. There are some young players who really understand that if you're here, enjoy it, but plant your seed to help this thing grow."

As if all of this wasn't enough, Staley now has an award named in her honor. Beginning in 2007, the WNBA will present the Dawn Staley Community Leadership Award to the player who best exemplifies the characteristics of a leader in the community in which she works or lives. Staley is appreciative of everything that has come her way. For her, it remains necessary that female athletes and basketball players share their experiences and share the good of the game.

According to Staley, the secret of success is really no secret: "Part of it is luck. Part of it is just working hard. Part of it is just being disciplined and being determined. It's difficult, but it isn't impossible to be successful in whatever you want to do."

In just seven seasons at the helm of the Temple University women's basketball team, Staley is well on her way to shaping the program into the national powerhouse that she promised when taking over on April 12, 2000. According to the Temple University Women's Basketball Media Guide,

The 2004 and 2005 Atlantic 10 Coach of the Year and 2005 Regional Coach of the Year, Staley has won 151 games, becoming the fastest coach in Temple women's basketball history to reach 100 wins. She has led the Owls to their first-ever A-10 Tournament titles (2002, 2004, 2005, 2006), five NCAA appearances since 2002 and a first-ever Top 25 National Ranking. In 2006 Temple won its third straight Atlantic 10 title, a feat that has been accomplished just one other time in A-10 history. The Owls have won four of the last six Conference titles. Staley has led the Owls to five NCAA Tournaments in her seven years at the helm. She is just one of two players in NCAA Tournament history to be voted the NCAA Final Four Outstanding Player and coach a team in the NCAA Tournament. The 2004 and 2005 Atlantic 10 Conference Coach of the Year and the 2001, 2002, 2005 and 2006 Philadelphia Big 5 Coach of the Year, Staley currently boasts a 151-67 record. She is also ranked 40th (latest rankings have not come out yet) on the list of winningest active head coaches (.693 winning percentage).[2]

"The Temple program hadn't reached the potential I thought it could," explained Staley. "It was a perfect fit because it allowed me to be near my family but also to embrace what college basketball is all about," said Staley.

Staley reflected on her years at Virginia, recognizing that her college experience allowed her to grow culturally and professionally and to broaden her horizons. That experience was so positive that Staley wanted to share it with her players at Temple. "I enjoy positively influencing players on a daily basis. That's what I enjoy most about coaching college basketball," said Staley. She also admits that playing the game at such a high level gives her better insights into coaching: "I truly believe I have a gift because not everyone sees the game they way I see the game. It also challenges me to help the players see what I see. When they do, it's a beautiful thing that unfolds because it's almost as if they're blind and I've taken the wool from over their eyes."

Staley regularly reminds her young players that while they may be talented, they are mere infants in the game. "I always tell my players that they are crawling right now, but by the time they leave Temple, they'll be running. They must be patient and disciplined and put the work in to get to all of those steps," she said.

Staley knows she has been blessed with the opportunity to play basketball, and she remains motivated and driven by challenges. Growing up in the projects of Philadelphia, Staley recalls a large field with a court on it. She remembers playing half-court basketball late at night as a young girl. "It always felt right to me. My love of basketball is innate. It just comes from a place deep inside my soul. I breathe it. I never tire of it. I embrace it. The answer is always yes. It never cheats. It's just a constant. It's a safe haven. Basketball is not my second nature. It's my first. I was born to play this game. I was born to share this game with other people. I've been given awards and rewards for playing this game. I don't let anything interfere with it. It's almost scary. Family, friends, or loved ones don't get in the way. They're second, and they know they're second."

When I asked Staley what other profession she would have entered, had she not been an athlete, she responded, "Gambling. Legalized gambling."

Dawn Staley is basketball royalty. Yet talking to her is like talking with any other player who loves the game in her heart and soul. Take little eleven-year-old Kristin from Nyack, New York. Kristin could be the next Dawn Staley. She loves the game with the same intensity, but what sets Staley apart from just about everyone else in the game is the combination of passion, talent, and work ethic. It remains to be seen if little Kristin or any other little girl out there can break any of Staley's records. If I learned anything at all in talking to Staley, one thing is for sure: if and when that day comes, Staley will be on hand to congratulate her.

Part six Media Coverage and Women's Basketball

13 The Slippery Slope of Gender Politics

etting access to a WNBA team is no piece of cake. When I embarked on this project, I was naive about the business of basketball, even though I knew that business existed. In order to watch a game live for the purposes of writing an article about that game or the players and coaches in the game, a press credential is required. This credential first provides the sports writer or photographer with a free seat at the game in the media section. It also provides access to locker rooms and media rooms prior to and after a game so that the writer or photographer can interview or photograph players and coaches. Further, a writer carrying a press credential also gains access to minute-by-minute statistics, media guides, and other reports produced typically by the home team. In order to find that credential, I pitched independent story ideas to print and Web magazines. I hit it off with the editor of *Full Court Press*, named Clay Kallam. His Web site is accessible by subscription only, so he was actually able to pay me a small amount per article. It wasn't much, but it was something in addition to a byline. Over the course of a summer, I came to trust Kallam's judgment and editorial skills. He, more than anyone else, taught me the ropes and helped me understand the business of the WNBA. Without his assistance I would not have received the proper press credentials to cover the games nor the savvy to navigate the tricky waters of a WNBA season.

With persistence I worked my way in and became accustomed to the routine. Typically I arrived at the arena two hours prior to tip-off. If the game was not at Madison Square Garden, I flew to the destination city the morning of the game and departed the morning following it. Once inside the arena, I signed in for the media credential and passed security checkpoints. Next I made my way to the pressroom to locate copies of everything from injury reports and game notes to team and league statistics to date. Then I checked the chart for my assigned seat. Although I typically sat courtside at all the Liberty's away games (thanks to the visiting team's public-relations staff), I never had particularly good seats at Madison Square Garden. Only the big-named daily publications are assigned regular seats on the floor (*New York Times*, *Daily News*, and so forth). Those writers not on a daily deadline with a mainstream publication are usually stuck like a bunch of illegitimate children in the press box at section 63. It's adjacent to the end of the Liberty's bench closer to the baseline, one section up. The view from the box is decent but far enough away to make you feel as though you're missing something important. Because we can't hear the courtside action or see the player's faces, all of us in the section 63 press box rely too heavily on the desktop monitors to show us replays and action from the far end of the court.

Shortly after the final buzzer sounds, the reporters in Section 63 move against traffic toward the courtside tunnel where the players enter and exit. Like salmon swimming upstream, we work our way slowly down the bleacher seating, silently allowing fans to shove us aside. Most of the other arenas I work in have a much easier and more organized access route for the media. It helps that they're all considerably newer than Madison Square Garden, but these little quirks make the Garden the magical place it is.

Once inside the tunnel, the press waits until the coaches make themselves available for questions. Usually the visiting coach answers questions in the hallway outside his or her team's locker room, while the home team's head coach typically has a media or interview room at his or her disposal. The writers are free to mill around and catch sound bytes from either coach or enter the locker rooms to talk with players. The locker rooms are open for only thirty minutes after the game ends. I learned the hard way in a preseason contest that if I spend thirty minutes listening to coaches in the press conferences, the locker rooms will be closed to the media by the time I'm ready to talk to the players. So now I jet to the locker rooms first and then to the coaches afterwards.

The mood inside the winning team's locker room is always conducive to interviews. Some players hit the showers first; others, usually the starters and captains, sit at their lockers in order to field questions.

Over the course of eighteen Liberty home games at Madison Square Garden in 2005, camaraderie developed among several of the writers in section 63. In addition to our assigned seats, we shared Liberty statistics and team rumors, more than a few laughs, and occasionally grabbed a pregame meal together. Most of the writers in section 63 were part-time writers or radio personalities. They each had full-time jobs but found a way write or commentate locally about the New York Liberty. Because print coverage in most daily newspapers is limited to the occasional 250-word Associated Press article, many loyal WNBA fans are forced to get their daily news about the season from Web-based sources, such as *Full Court Press*.

Unlike most of the other writers, who usually spent their pregames busy eating, working, or hanging out in the pressroom, I typically spent the entire pregame in the arena watching the players shoot around. Because ticket holders are not allowed in the arena until forty-five minutes before tipoff, the arena seats are mine to choose from. This long before the game starts, the players are relaxed, and the arena is quiet. The players know there aren't any fans watching or any cameras on them, so they joke around, laugh with one another, and go about the business of warming up.

For me this is the real game of basketball—the rituals and warm-ups, the mental preparation, and the team camaraderie. While the game is showtime, the moments before the opening buzzer are the ones I can relate to the most. The drills are familiar, the staccato of the passing and dribbling in unison, the laughing, and the stretching are all as familiar to me as my own breathing. Yet the place the players go to upon tipoff, however vaguely familiar it may be in my dreams, remains foreign to me.

The only other part of the game experience I find to be almost as meaningful is the playing of the national anthem prior to tipoff. As hokey as that sounds, it's true. The actual performance matters little. From city to city, from my youth to my present, it remains my moment to close my eyes and stand with the players on the sidelines. I can feel the energy and the crowd around me in the same way the players must. Every time, it gives me the chills.

In these quiet moments the magic of the game takes hold of me once again. No matter how close I get to the players on the court or how much I concentrate and digest statistics or follow plays and diagrams, I am not one of them. I am not a player. I am no longer a teammate or a captain. As the years pass, that disappointment has never lessened.

I had hoped that by coming back to the game in this manner, I would plug the hole left in my life by basketball. I would somehow accept my role as a transcriber of the action, a voice for it but not a participant in it. Yet, I am quietly learning that I will never end the daydreaming or stop the wishing. I realize now that I will become an old woman who still dreams of flying down the court with the number fifteen on my back.

Even with the tremendous growth in the area of female athletics, I learned firsthand during this past summer that the concept of progress within gender politics in the sport media matrix is debatable. Growing up in rural Connecticut in the late 1970s, I realized early-on the tomboy stigma of being a girl and athletic, and I lived with it. However, when I began my coverage of the New York Liberty basketball team in 2005, it did not occur to me that so few women would be reporting on the WNBA or sports in general.

Each city I traveled to, each arena I entered, men overwhelmingly populated each press box I sat in. In many instances these male sports writers usually covered the NHL or the NBA, but because neither league played in the summer months, the WNBA became their meal ticket. I also found a large number of extremely young sports writers who had no real interest in covering the WNBA as a career. They wrote articles about the WNBA because their editors wanted them to practice their skills in order to make the "jump" to men's professional sports. In the first round of the Eastern Conference Playoffs in 2005, I sat next to a *New York Times* freelance writer who could not properly pronounce the New York Liberty's All-Star captain's last name. He had no idea what position she played or how the Liberty had performed all season, yet he was writing an article about the Liberty for the *New York Times*.

Of course this leads to the male-dominated argument that female athletics is a second-class citizen in the world of sports. It's acceptable for a writer to make mistakes in covering the women's games so long as he learns from those mistakes before he begins covering the men. David Salter wrote in his book *Crashing the Old Boys' Network: The Tragedies and Triumphs of Girls and Women in Sports*: "One way to look at it is that society has taught young boys for centuries that to be female is to be second class."[1] Why should the realm of sports writing be any different?

Marie Hardin, associate director of research at the Center for Sports Journalism at Penn State University, studies the subject of women in the sports media every day. She said, "Coverage encourages interest. Coverage tells people this is important, and you should pay attention. If things are not covered, then people will assume it is not important and not interesting. We don't yet know if there was more coverage of women's sports, whether or not people would then pay attention. Because then the interest would feed on itself."

Hardin believes that newspaper editors may say that their readership is not interested in women's sports, yet they don't have empirical evidence to prove this beyond the phone calls and e-mails that they get. Some chalk it up to a simple equation: the sports editors themselves are not supporters of women's sports, so therefore coverage of women's sports is low. However, according to Hardin, the real problem is the beat system: "It is complicated because sports departments are run on beat systems. There aren't many women's sports that call for a beat, aside from the WNBA and certain women's college sports. We need more professional sports leagues to get women's beats in newsrooms normalized. If you don't have beat coverage of a sport, it's sort of catch as catch can, and it means that the programs never really develop a regular following because they can't get regular coverage."

Donna Lopiano, former CEO of the Women's Sports Foundation, keeps close eye on media coverage of women's basketball. She said, "There is research that shows that the decisions about what goes into a newspaper depends on the preferences of the sports editor. These decisions are not based on data or consumer preference but rather the preferences and bias of the sports editor. So when you have a profession like sports journalism that is less than 10 percent female, and sports editors are predominantly male, that's a recipe, at least in the print media, for what you get. It's probably a little worse in the electronic media."

Lopiano believes that coverage of women's sports has actually gone backwards in the last ten years, and she doesn't think there is any reason to believe that coverage will change soon: "I think it's going to take a change in leadership or a public outcry that puts pressure on newspapers. A consistent, concerted effort to express consumer displeasure is something that is difficult to sustain. I wish I had better news."

As a woman, I felt an extreme pressure to ask the correct questions and handle myself as professionally as possible, although I did not see the same level of seriousness from the men. If I misspoke or did not adequately know the facts in a particular situation or game, I was unceremoniously told so and ignored by my male counterparts. It was as if I was held to a higher standard because I was a woman writing about sports. David Salter asserts in *Crashing the Old Boys' Network* that "there may be no other situation in which a woman is challenged more frequently and more vehemently by men than sports writing and sports casting."[2]

Time and time again, I saw male sportswriters relay incorrect facts and make sexist comments from the sidelines. Judy Goldstein from the *Houston Chronicle* made the statement, "Men don't rub off on each other. If a man does something idiotic, it reflects on him and him only. Unfortunately, if a woman mishandles herself, it reflects on all other women."

Most of Marie Hardin's research is with women's sports journalists, and she believes my experience to be pretty typical in the realm of sports coverage: "Women are entering the field of sports journalism, but it is a revolving door."

According to David Salter, "Since the first female sports journalist made her debut in the early 1970s, no group has been met with more resistance. Men have felt all along that women sports journalists simply do not have the knowledge to report on the topic."[3] With regard to women's professional sports, who better to provide media coverage than a woman who has played and experienced what it is like to be female and an athlete in our society?

In July of 2005 I covered the WNBA's annual All-Star Game at the Mohegan Sun Arena in Connecticut. The 9,168 fans at the sold-out Mohegan Sun Arena were raucous and lively. As a woman and female athlete, I experienced at court level over nine thousand men, women, and children cheering for ten women on a basketball court. The environment was electric and based not on the athletes' physical attractiveness, but on competition. Having the opportunity to cover the game as a member of the working press filled me with tremendous pride. I doubt any of the male sportswriters present had, or ever could have, the same reaction to the experience because there is a difference between the way a woman and her male counterparts will cover sports. Liz Kahn, a freelancer in London who writes for the *Daily Telegraph, the Guardian,* and the *Mail on Sunday,* said in a recent interview, "I think women generally have a wider perspective. Women are more interested in the emotional makeup of a person, they're more interested in their motivation, in the psychological aspect of the sport than a man is, and that probably comes out in their writing."[4]

Donna Lopiano feels that right now there is very little overlap between those who watch men's sports versus those who watch women's sports. Her sense is if you're into physical contact, strength, violence, you watch men's sports. If you're into men's baseball or women's skills sports, which basketball is, you're probably going to watch women's sports. Women's sports are more family oriented, more "grandma friendly," than men's sports, which are more corporate oriented in terms of who buys the tickets. Men's sports are also very blue-collar oriented. She said, "Women's sports are still suffering from lack of critical mass because it's only the forty-five-year-old-and-under viewer who is the Title IX baby male and female who have grown up respecting women and sport and who watch women's basketball. You still have half the population who grew up in a culture with an old-fashioned view of femininity and sport." Lopiano believes that stereotyped views of women and sport will die off over time.

Furthermore, it's important to understand some statistics and ratios when discussing sports coverage. Margaret Carlisle Duncan and Michael Messner studied sports coverage on three network affiliates in Los Angeles in their report, *Gender in Televised Sports: News and Highlights Shows, 1989–2004,* which was done for the Amateur Athletic Foundation of Los Angeles. They reported that only 9 percent of airtime was devoted to women's sports in contrast to the 88 percent devoted to male athletes. Females fared even worse on ESPN's national sports show *Sports Center,* where they occupied just over 2 percent of airtime. There were many broadcasts that contained no coverage of women's sports whatsoever. Well over half (58 percent) of the network-affiliate news shows included no women's sports stories and 48 percent of the Fox and ESPN highlight shows included no women's sports stories. Meanwhile, 100 percent of the same sampling included coverage of men's sports. There were 28.8 times as many column inches devoted to men-only sports stories as there were to women-only sport stories, with only 3.2 percent of front-page stories focusing on women-only sports.[5]

Marie Hardin from Penn State University does think coverage will increase but only by a relatively small margin. More women in the sports journalism field won't necessarily translate into more coverage of women's sports. Simply put the women's sports beat is the lowest beat on the rung. If you're serious about a career in sports journalism, the last assignment you want is the women's sports beat. Hardin said, "Women's sports coverage continues to be ghettoized, and female journalists will continue to run from it unless things change. Women's sports journalists will not gain more respect in the sports department until women's sports gains more respect."

Doris Burke, a basketball analyst with ESPN, did not enter the sports commentating business intentionally. After covering the Providence Lady Friars on the radio, Burke was offered an opportunity with ESPN. Burke recalls entering the business of covering women's basketball on television. She said, "When I first came into the business, I was strictly a color analyst. Until the WNBA was formed in 1997, women could not make a living as a color analyst doing strictly what a Dick Vitale or a Bill Raftery do to make a living. The WNBA afforded me that opportunity."

Michael Messner made the point in his book titled *Taking the Field: Women, Men, and Sports* that "the enthusiasm for women's sports is expanding too quickly for the imagery of women athletes to be totally and continually ghettoized." Messner believes there are four patterned ways the dominant sports media deal with women's sports: silence, humorous sexualization, backlash, and selective incorporation of standout women athletes.[6]

With the growing acceptance of female athletes and women in sports throughout American society, it is no surprise that the overall picture of women in sports media is one of growth. Organizations such as the Association of Women in Sport Media more than doubled their membership from 400 to 850 between 1994 and 2000.[7] Perceptions of what actually constitutes progress in an industry where men outnumber women at a ratio of nearly eight to one appears to vary considerably from one practitioner to another.

Margaret Duncan and Michael Messner concluded in *Gender in Televised Sports* that there was a

> huge statistical difference in the quantity of men's and women's stories, the total number of column inches, and the number of photographs of male and female athletes. They were encouraged by the example of *USA Today*, a newspaper that sells more than 1.3 million copies a day. *USA Today* had more women's stories than any other paper in the sample. In fact, *USA Today* published 43.5 percent of all women-only stories. There is hope that the media landscape will change, albeit slowly.

It is still not clear if the WNBA can become financially solvent in a social climate still unable to grasp true equality with regard to sports and media coverage. E. J. Staurowsky asserted in *Women and Men in the Press Box: The Price of Progress* that "one way to measure genuine progress is to consider the question of whether the sport media culture, at an ideological level, has ventured far from its roots in a male supremacist view of the world to embrace a concept of women and men as fundamentally equal. Because of its historical significance, an examination of the ways in which women have been banned and/or discouraged from working in sport media provides some insight in this regard."[8]

While all of this social construction and reconstruction is occurring, the fact is women continue to participate in sports at an increasing rate each year. The male-dominated media spectrum still too often trivializes and sexualizes the female athlete. With a few exceptions, women's sports still struggle to find any kind of footing on the national, or even local, sports pages. The average consumer can review the local sports page and notice few if any articles focused on women's sports. The fact is the Anna Kournikova syndrome still very much exists. The Russian tennis star is one of the few female athletes to ever grace the cover of *Sports Illustrated*, despite never winning a tennis tournament. As more and more girls and women are allowed access to sports, the hope is that at some point these female athletes, these consumers and audiences, will force the market, and ultimately the editors, to keep pace.

14 Unique but Alike

The happiest, purest form of inspiration and confidence I have ever experienced is found on the basketball court. Deep within me I feel the pure magic, the sheer, unabashed joy of a high arching fadeaway, a perfect pick and roll, or a flawless box-out. When I cross over the threshold and step out onto a gym floor, I'm able to shut the world out completely and leave my introverted shell for forty minutes to become a vocal, outspoken leader who is capable of scoring at will, who is capable of winning games and making my teammates better than they thought they could be.

You would think that delight would be noticeable to everyone, would be cause for celebration and admiration. Yet, there was no fanfare in my final competitive basketball game. No marching bands. No autographs. I recall we lost the game to

John Jay. It was a cold night, with heavy rains and gusty winds. The gym at John Jay School of Criminal Justice was old. The floorboard creaked, and the locker rooms stunk of mildew. This was as far from the lights of the big time as one could get. My college team should have won that game and we didn't. I recall scoring my average fifteen or twenty points, but I did not lead my team to a win. That night I walked from the dank locker rooms to the bus and stopped at the empty court to say goodbye. This had been my final night to lace up the sneakers and fly. It was the end of eighteen years of sweat and hard work. It was the end of double sessions and suicides, memorizing playbooks, and nursing injuries. Several years later in an attempt to fill the gaping hole that basketball left, I joined a women's league at the Chelsea Piers in Manhattan. I was totally out of shape and had not picked up a ball in almost three years.

I began in the league quietly, rushing from my job at a Manhattan public-relations firm to the Piers at night. Intimidated by the street feel of the games, I kept to myself. Little by little I became reacquainted with the game I desperately missed. After the first two weeks, I realized something new. I found that while I was struggling to get up and down the floor, I was smarter. Although I had not played ball in some time, I had continued to watch it on TV and listen to it on the radio. Those years did not go without learning. It's called basketball IQ, and mine was at Mensa levels. I was smarter on the court than anyone else. I sized up players' strengths and weaknesses. I knew who liked what spot and where I could be the most effective. I could speed the game up in my mind and predict the movements of the players like the orbit of the moon. Game by game, I gained confidence.

I don't remember much about that league. I don't recall specific games or plays. I do, however, remember some of the championship game. Our team had made it to the league finals. I can't tell you any of my teammates' names. I wouldn't be able to recognize any of them on the streets. I don't even remember the final score, but I do know we won by one point at the buzzer. I also recall being totally on fire. By the time the final buzzer sounded, I had scored well over forty points, with at least ten rebounds and ten assists. I was unstoppable. A crowd had gathered to watch me play, point me out, and cheer me on. The basketball director at the Chelsea Piers told me, "Hell, I've seen a lot of players—guys and girls—come through these doors. In my years here, no one ever played a game like that."

My teammates presented the championship trophy to me as we unlaced our sneakers and downed some water. It was my shot that propelled us to a win in the final seconds of the game, although I can't tell you if it was a two or a three or where it was on the court. Everyone told me I looked completely possessed, that they were amazed by my performance and my will to win.

The trophy was at least four feet tall—definitely overkill for a local league. I gave it to some kid on the city bus who said he would love to have a trophy that big in his room. I didn't care about the league or the trophy. I recall telling myself there was no way in hell I was going to lose the game, but that anger subsided the moment the game ended. Instead of elation I felt sadness. Actually my performance made me almost sick. Sick that I could string a game like that together and be twenty pounds overweight. Sick that I had stepped away from the game for three years and could still dominate. It made me want to curl up in a ball and sleep away the next fifty years like Rip Van Winkle because then I would not spend another day wondering if I could have made it at a higher level.

The reality is, just as the NCAA advertises, most of the NCAA scholar athletes go on to do something else other than play sports. Jody Conradt, former University of Texas head coach talked about the life lessons that basketball teaches. New UT head coach Gail Goestenkors mentioned how many companies actively recruit former NCAA team athletes because student athletes don't shy away from hard work and because they work well within a team dynamic. All this may be true, but for some the end of our playing days is painful and not something we ever really get over. Some lucky few have the knack for color commentating or describing game action as it unfolds.

Doris Burke has been, and continues to be, a female pioneer in the broadcasting world.

On February 9, 2000, she became the first woman to serve as an analyst for a New York Knicks basketball game on MSG Network, and she continues to serve in a back-up capacity for TV and radio. In 1999–2000, she became the first woman hired as a regular commentator for a men's basketball package when she did games for the Atlantic-10. Burke is also a regular contributor to ESPN NCAA, NBA and the WNBA as a game studio analyst. Over the past several years, Burke has called NCAA Tournament games, conference tournaments, All-American games, NIT games, and in-season games for ESPN.

In 1990, Providence became the first New England school to broadcast women's basketball on commercial radio and the natural choice for the analyst spot was Burke. She began calling basketball games on New England Sports Network (NESN) in 1990. The following season she worked some men's games on NESN and was tabbed by ESPN for the NCAA Division II Championship. In 1992, she became the analyst of Big East women's basketball on television and called a pair of Providence men's games on radio as well. In 1993, Burke served as analyst for the Penn State Television Network and began to take on an expanded broadcasting role at ESPN. In 1995, she worked as analyst on the Atlantic-10's women's package and served as analyst for the ECAC men's and women's games of the week. That same year, she became the first woman ever to call a Big East Conference men's game while working the Big East Game of the Week from Providence.[1]

Burke entered the realm of commentating by accident. She left coaching at Providence when she became engaged. Knowing that she wanted a family quickly after being married, the schedule of a Division I coach just didn't fit into her equation. "While I've known many women able to maintain the balance between being a mom and being a coach at that level, I did not think that I could be one of those people," said Burke.

When Providence offered her a chance to commentate their women's games on radio, it sounded intriguing to Burke, and she gave it a try. "I had a birds-eye view of the action. I was still able to interact with the players on some level, which I took great joy in. I was still part of a game that had shaped me from the earliest parts of my life," said Burke.

Although Burke sees countless basketball courts in countless cities across the countries, she still remembers a small park near her childhood home: "I spent a good portion of my childhood in that little park pounding a basketball. The game is in my blood and remains a great shaping force in my life to this point."

Burke realizes that her initial experience in broadcasting was so positive because it afforded her the chance to be around the game she loved so much. For her, the game of basketball shaped her and continues to shape her. Her time at Providence College as a part of the women's basketball team was also a defining time for her. "There are many opportunities in life to compete, but to do it at a Division I basketball institution like Providence is an experience that's hard to reproduce after you've left college," said Burke.

College basketball is something special for Burke. According to her, there are nuances to competing for at the intercollegiate level. The student athletes are young and still in their formative stages, still becoming who they will become. Student athletes constantly strive to maintain that balance between athletic and academic life. "There is enormous pride taken in representing the institution for which you play. I miss that. I remain a Friar to this day, and I am incredibly thankful for my experiences there. I will always be indebted to Providence College and the Big East for affording me a chance to compete at the highest level," said Burke. She is quick to point out that she misses the people, she misses the games, and she misses the camaraderie in the locker room.

Burke's most vivid basketball memory came her junior year at Providence when the Friars took the Big East regular season championship. "The year prior, we went 16-16. Having a .500 record felt like the end of the world. It was one of the longest periods of my life. It was just miserable. We didn't win much, we weren't very good, and we didn't enjoy it at all," recalled Burke.

However, in her junior season Bob Foley became the new head coach, convincing Burke and her teammates in a very short span of time that they could rise from one of the worst teams in the Big East Conference to one of the best. "The process of that turnaround was really special," said Burke.

While Burke loves to be around the game day in and day out, the travel aspect of her job leaves a little to be desired. She believes there is a romantic view of sports television analysts. "I have struggled with the travel from the outset. It can be monotonous. People have a false perception of what life is really like for a television sports commentator. They think you spend all your time with elite athletes, and they imagine how cool it is," said Burke. While she maintains joy in her job, she admits that there is an element of tedium: "I see the hotel and the gym and nothing more."

Although there are drawbacks to life on the road, Burke explained that the good outweighs the bad: "I stay involved in a game I love so much. It's afforded me the chance to watch the women's college game go from a relative unknown to an important part of the sports landscape." Burke suggests that people evaluate performance of sports in terms of ratings. Now the WNBA and NCAA get solid ratings, and she's pleased to be a part of that progression.

Further, Burke absolutely loves to be around such talented players and coaches. "I cover men's and women's NCAA basketball, and I'm allowed to interact with the Mike Krzyzewskis, the Pat Summitts and Mary Williams of the game. Not only are they knowledgeable basketball people, but also by and large they are incredibly good human beings who have an incredible work ethic to achieve a certain status." Burke believes that being around successful people makes you motivated to work harder and do all those things you're able to do, and she's right. One can't help but be motivated and inspired when one talks with basketball legend turned broadcaster and writer, Nancy Lieberman.

Hall of Famer Nancy Lieberman is an accomplished basketball player, coach, two time Olympian, broadcaster, and writer. She is one of the most recognized individuals in the history of women's basketball. Lieberman's inspirational journey is a story of determination, strength, and incredible motivation to become the greatest. A native of Queens, New York, playing hoops on the rough-and-tumble Harlem courts, Nancy Lieberman developed a tough style of basketball that led her on a remarkable basketball journey.

Lieberman recalled being in the fourth or fifth grade at PS104 when she saw some boys on a basketball court. She stopped at the small gym and picked up a ball. She remembers being intrigued by the game at that age: "I thought, this is interesting." A few nights later Lieberman watched the Knicks play the Bucks on television. The next morning as she did her chores around the house, she remembers being in awe that the score was in the 100s.

Years later when she was played pickup ball in Queens, she was picked regularly, regardless of the fact that she was a girl. "We played one-on-one, two-on-two, three-on-three the majority of the time. It got to the point that if you got picked, that was status on the streets. I was one of those players who was routinely getting picked to play. It made me feel good. Instead of people asking, why are you playing? where did we go wrong, girls don't play sports?, these black guys—white guys, it didn't matter—they were pretty much saying we want you. It was very much a part of my confidence and my self-esteem. It made me feel great that I was wanted," recalled Lieberman.

In 1974 while attending Far Rockaway High School, she established herself as one of the top women's basketball players in the country by earning one of only twelve slots on the USA's national team. Playing USA Basketball was a great starting point for Lieberman because getting picked gave her confidence to know she was skilled. She was fifteen years old when she first tried out in 1974 for her first USA team. "I went to Queens College for a regional tryout on a lark with a friend of mine. They gave each player a number, and they kept eliminating. We started in the early morning, and by the end of the day I was still there. I'd look on the wall to see if my number was there, and I couldn't believe my number was there. My mother asked where I was and I said, 'I'm just playing ball, I'll be home later,'" said Lieberman.

After that initial tryout, Lieberman attended a camp where

they narrowed players down to a final roster of twelve. "Ann Meyers, Pat Summit, Dottie McKray, and all the studs in women's basketball who were ultimately going to be my future teammates were there. I kept calling home, and my brother kept saying, 'Can you believe you're playing?' I was fifteen playing against twenty-year-olds," said Lieberman.

At five feet six inches, Lieberman could dunk a tennis ball. No one had really seen that kind of athleticism in the women's game. "I played like a boy. I was very physical, very aggressive. Some of my teammates or opponents would get upset with the way I played, but I didn't know any other way to play except how people had played against me, which were the guys, and they were very strong, very physical, and very intimidating, and that became my game," said Lieberman. The following year, Lieberman was named to the USA team designated to play in the World Championships and Pan American Games where she brought home a gold metal in 1975 and a silver medal in 1979. In the 1976 Summer Olympics in Montreal, she became the youngest basketball player in Olympic history to win a silver medal at the age of eighteen.

Lieberman said of her Olympic experience, "Winning the silver medal at the 1976 Olympics was amazing. It was the first time women's basketball was ever in the Olympics. I don't know how many people know this, but we didn't have a budget. No one thought we were going to medal. We had to attend a pre-Olympic tournament in Hamilton, Ontario, to qualify for Montreal. When we qualified, Bill Wall, who was really the father of women's basketball and USA Basketball, he and Billy Jean Moore had to put our travel expenses on their personal credit cards because no one thought the U.S. team had a chance to qualify. When I look back, it's amazing that happened. We went to Montreal. We stunned everyone winning the silver medal."

Lieberman recalls being in the locker room prior to that game. She had just turned eighteen. "Billy Jean Moore, our head coach, said, 'Ladies, this is a very significant game. It's not just a game. What you do today will impact the future of women's basketball for the next twenty-five years.' When you're eighteen years old, and someone is sitting there telling you that you're going to impact the game for the next twenty-five years, you have no clue what she's talking about. You live in the now. You can't even remember what you had for dinner yesterday, and she's telling me this is going to change women's basketball?"

Years later Lieberman finally understands the real meaning of that speech. She said, "She was absolutely right. Our success changed women's basketball on so many levels. There were so many life lessons I learned from that game. It changed my life; it changed all of our lives."

From 1976 to 1980 Lieberman attended Old Dominion University in Norfolk, Virginia where she and her team won two consecutive Association for Intercollegiate Athletics for Women National Championships (1979, 1980) and compiled a 72-2 record. Lieberman played with Anne Donovan at ODU for one season in 1980 and also lead the Lady Monarchs to a National Women's Invitation Tournament (WNIT) Championship in 1978.

Lieberman's life changed drastically after capturing the silver medal in Montreal because of the extraordinary amount of exposure she received. Old Dominion was nicknamed America's team because games would sell out or have record attendance in every city Lieberman and her teammates played. All of it was due to Lieberman's experience in the Olympic Games. "Think about it, everyone else was gone. I was the only one who went on to play in college. Pat Summit went to Tennessee to coach. I truly appreciate the opportunities in the fact that my timing was good, but it helped women's basketball and that was the most important thing," Lieberman said.

Lieberman was the first two-time winner of the prestigious Wade Trophy, a national player of the year award in college women's basketball, and was selected as the Broderick Award winner for basketball as the top women's player in America. Lieberman also won three consecutive Kodak All-America awards (1978, 1979, 1980). Lieberman's storied career at ODU included 2,430 points, 1,167 rebounds, 983 assists, and over 700 steals in just 134 games.

At the professional level, Lieberman played for several basketball teams and leagues, including the Dallas Diamonds of the Women's Pro Basketball League (WBL), eventually the Women's

American Basketball Association (WABA), where she led the team to the 1984 WABA Championship. She led in scoring and won the league's MVP award. In 1986 Lieberman became the first women ever to play in a men's league; she played for the Springfield Fame in the United States Basketball League (USBL) and also with the Washington Generals.

She was elected to the Basketball Hall of Fame as a player in 1996 and to the Women's Basketball Hall of Fame in 1999. "It is the single most wonderful moment, when you play this game to play, because it is a game," Lieberman said of her Hall of Fame induction. "When after twenty years, the game says thank you to you for playing it, for playing it with integrity and spirit and inspiration. That might be the most poignant moment of my life as an athlete because it meant that you had impact on your sport. I dearly love women's basketball and basketball in general."

In January 1997 Lieberman was drafted in the inaugural season by the Women's National Basketball Association's (WNBA), for the Phoenix Mercury, at the age of thirty-eight. During her professional career, Lieberman averaged 15.7 points, 6.4 rebounds, and 6.1 assists per game.

In 2000 she returned to Old Dominion University to complete her undergraduate degree in interdisciplinary studies. At the time she had been serving as president of the Women's Sports Foundation. In 2004 she became the head coach for the Dallas Fury of the National Women's Basketball League and guided the team to a championship that season."

Annually the Nancy Lieberman Award is given to the best female point guard in Division I basketball. Previous winners included Sue Bird, Diana Taurasi, Temeka Johnson, and Ivory Latta.

Over the years Lieberman has seen a change in the attitudes of the younger players. "A few years ago, I attended the Nike Skills Academy with juniors in high school. I walked in the arena and saw life-size banners of the players hanging from the ceiling like these kids were five-time Olympians. I remember thinking these kids haven't done a stinking thing yet. Teresa Edwards was with me. We never had a picture of ourselves hanging in a building like these, and these are only juniors in high school," said Lieberman. She's not surprised that young athletes turn into egomaniacs because all the hype and promotion makes them into egomaniacs. "Times have changed. There's more media, more exposure, more opportunities, more is given, and more is taken. It's a delicate balance," said Lieberman.

Lieberman has a bird's-eye view of the hype and promotion and its affect on young athletes: "Lieberman has provided commentary for ABC, ESPN, NBC, and contributing writer to the *Dallas Morning News*, the *New York Times* and *USA Today*. She is currently a full-time analyst with ESPN for men's and women's college basketball and both the men's (NBA) and women's (WNBA) National Basketball Association's development leagues. Instead of taking time off during the summer, she coaches women basketball camps in Dallas, Detroit and Phoenix. She has authored several books and videotapes. Her first book, published in 1991, is her autobiography entitled Lady Magic: The Nancy Lieberman Story. She later co-authored her second book Basketball for Women."[2] This experience has provided her a unique perspective on the game and her place in it.

"It changed the course of the history of the game through the opportunities that were afforded me," Lieberman explained. "That's never been lost on me, my role or the role that I was given in the big picture. I'm really proud of it."

Lieberman just loves the game, the freedom, the split-second decision making, the creativity. "When you're going from offense to defense, and you have that transition and you have to rethink instantaneously, that's what I love. You don't get a chance to go to the huddle and think it through, make a pass, think it through again. You have to react, and react quickly. I might want to shoot a jumper, but it might not be there. I might have to resituate as it's unfolding. I so fell in love with the freedom—it's almost like ballet in the air. That's the funny thing. I can go on a basketball court and be free to make moves that I never thought I could do—footwork and balance, aesthetic beauty, spinning in the air, contorting my body, being totally uninhibited, but put me on a dance floor, and I'm scared to death. I always used to say I'm like a kid in a sandbox. It's the safest place. If you put me between ninety-four [feet] and fifty [feet], it is the safest place I have ever felt in my life. It's always been a safety net. Whenever I had my fears or apprehensions, I would go play," said Lieberman.

In 1998 she was hired as general manager and head coach of the WNBA's Detroit Shock, a team she coached for three seasons. When Lieberman took the job coaching in Detroit, she had never coached before and was apprehensive. "I couldn't sleep because I had so much to think about. It wasn't unusual to find me at the practice facility at two or three o'clock in the morning just bouncing the ball, shooting, or working through my thoughts. When I came back to play in 1997 in the WNBA at age thirty-nine, people didn't think I could do it."

The next words out of Lieberman's mouth made me think I was talking to myself. She said, "The safest place for me was to get between the lines on the court, it's always been so comforting." That's when it hit me—I mean really hit me. After talking with players and coaches at just about every level of the game, after studying statistics and listening to some of the greatest minds in women's sports talk about the importance of a core audience, the importance of reaching a consumer group of former athletes, it all came down to one simple realization: there are just some players who feel the game deep in their souls. Once that connection is forged, it can never be broken. It is as real as the pillow under our heads at night, as certain as knowing our birthdates. It is, quite simply, what makes us so incredibly unique and so incredibly alike.

15 Her Place of Peace

On September 10, 2005, I sat in the Indiana Fever's Conseco Fieldhouse pressroom prior to Game 3 in the first round of the Eastern Conference Playoffs. In this second game of a best-of-three series, Indiana had the upper hand. One more win for them would end the series and send the Liberty back to New York. The smallest crowd in Indiana franchise history (5,085) was on hand to witness the Fever win their first-ever bid to the Eastern Conference Finals by snuffing out the New York Liberty 58–50.

New York came out of the gate flat, scoring only sixteen points in the first half, the third fewest points in a half of a WNBA playoff game. The Liberty not only shot poorly, but they also finished with a whopping eleven turnovers in the first half alone. Watching the first half was like watching a train wreck.

For the first time all season, I took few notes and even heard myself cheer once or twice when they scored, even though the unwritten rule for any sports writer is to never take sides. By the end of the first half, not one Liberty player looked like they expected to win that game, and everyone in the arena knew it was over.

After the game the press was escorted to a spacious media room where postgame interviews were held. Because this was the playoffs, the WNBA, rather than the individual team, controlled the postgame process. NBA-TV covered the postgame interviews, so there was a substantial crew in the back of the room setting up two different television cameras and the related sound equipment. Instead of milling around, the press was told to stay put while players and coaches from both teams entered the room to take questions.

First, winning coach Brian Winters stepped up to the podium. Perhaps ten or fifteen writers and photographers populated the room. Coach Winters was subdued after his team's historic win. "It wasn't a pretty game, that's for sure, but our defense was terrific tonight and we managed to stay poised enough to hit a few shots," he said. Following Winters, Indiana's Tamika Catchings stepped in. Catchings said, "We've grown a lot as a team. One of our goals was to make it to the conference finals and to contend for a championship. We're doing that and it feels great. Overall we missed a lot of easy shots, but we regrouped on defense."

When Catchings left the room, about half of the press also took their exit. A few more trickled out waiting for Liberty head coach Pat Coyle. After a few minutes Coyle entered the large pressroom that now contained only three other writers besides me. As usual Coyle had few words to express her team's season-ending loss. She said, "Indiana is a good team, and they're playing well. It's a good time to play well. Let's leave it at that." She also expressed some displeasure at how few writers were present. Perhaps they, like me, had learned the lesson that she never said much we could use.

After Coyle's remarks the other two remaining writers left the room, leaving me alone with two Indiana Fever staffers and the NBA-TV crew. I stood up to leave, knowing full well a player from

New York was expected, because it just didn't make sense for me to be the only writer in the room. The Fever staffers asked me to stay because they needed the Liberty player's quotes for the record, but they also needed a member of the media to ask the questions. So I waited, completely uncomfortable and unsure.

In walked a somber Becky Hammon. Hammon's eyes scanned the room. No doubt she was already upset by the loss, but the empty media room clearly irked her. She raised her eyebrows as if to say, "OK, let's get this over quickly." I realized it was my chance to ask questions—my only chance to speak with her—but instead of the quiet personal interview I had always envisioned, this one came complete with national television cameras and a microphone. While I wanted to ask her so many questions about her life and basketball, I also wanted to be professional and do what was expected of me. Adding to my fear was something Hammon said to me once: "A lot of it is timing on when to talk to me. After I just lost, it's probably not a good time to come at me." I was afraid of exactly that.

Hammon added fourteen points on five of eleven shooting but finished with five turnovers (four in the first half) and only three assists. I asked her what went wrong for New York. She said, "We were frustrated, but I think we looked up at the score-board and we couldn't play it any worse; we were only down ten or eleven [points]. That's not a feat that's impossible for us, and we crawled back in it. The problem was when you bury yourself like that on the road, you exert so much energy just to get back in it that everything has to go your way those last minutes to get over that hump. When we did make our surge, we just didn't have enough to finish it off. We knew going into the locker room we couldn't play any worse, so let's go out and leave it all out there. With us shots are going to fall. It's not a matter of if they'll fall but when."

The Liberty ended their 2005 season with eighteen wins and seventeen losses, after losing in the first round of the playoffs for the first time in franchise history. I asked Hammon what she thought her team did well this season and what she was looking at building on. She replied quietly, her voice conveying how tired and frustrated she was by the loss: "That's a tough question because my mind is still reeling about this last game. Overall I thought we were up and down, as were a lot of other teams. You never knew what team was going to show up on what night. When I look back at what we did well, we had a lot of young players come in and help us. We're just going to have to get better in the off season. We play unselfishly, we defend well, we shoot well. But our Achilles heel has been offensive rebounding, and that came back to hurt us tonight."

I thanked Hammon for her time, and she left the room. Walking back down the tunnel ahead of me, I overheard her talking with the Liberty's public-relations manager about her plans to spend some time with family in Connecticut. She looked exhausted. I knew she had no idea how significant an event that was for me in my life and my journey. I doubt she has any recollection of me or of my questions. I had learned how to blend into the woodwork of the working press.

Back on April 24, 2005, in my first interaction with the New York Liberty as a member of the media, I wished to speak with Hammon the most. At the time she was a cocaptain. She was the soul of their team. I finally got the chance on an unseasonably warm late October afternoon in 2006, months before the trade that would send her to San Antonio. During this conversation, however, there were no cameras or podiums.

Becky has emerged on the WNBA scene as not only one of the most popular personalities in the league but also one of the top players. A native of Rapid City, South Dakota, she was the first woman from South Dakota to play in the WNBA and began her rise to stardom for the Rapid City Stevens High School Raiders. She was named Gatorade South Dakota Player of the Year in 1995 and South Dakota Ms. Basketball in 1994.

At Colorado State University (CSU), Hammon led the Rams to their first NCAA Tournament appearance in 1997 and to a Sweet Sixteen appearance in 1999. Her career at CSU found her in the record books for points (2,740), points per game (21.9), field goals made (918), and assists (538).

Hammon recalled her four years at CSU. She said, "Some of my best, most precious moments were in college, at Colorado State. What my teammates and coaches did there was very special to me. Going from a team that was sub-.500 to winning twenty-plus games, being ranked fourth or fifth in the country my senior year, was a pretty phenomenal story."

Hammon doesn't think people quite understand the magnitude of that progression. "My freshman year, we only had about two hundred people in the stands, on a good night. By my senior year, we were selling out a week in advance. I have a special place in my heart for Fort Collins and all the people of Colorado."

Over the course of eight seasons with the Liberty, Hammon not only became a starting point guard but also became a WNBA superstar known for her grit and scoring potency. For Hammon being named an All-Star for the first time in 2003, after she had blown out her knee, was an extremely special moment in her basketball career. She said, "The coaches voted to put me on the team even though I was unable to play. That was really special to me."

In 2006, after a significant retooling of the roster by general manager Carol Blazejowski, the Liberty finished the season out of playoff contention with a record of a disappointing 11-23. Hammon was the only returning starter left on the Liberty squad.

Hammon said of her disappointing 2006 season, "I knew going in it was going to be a challenge, we had a lot of new people. I wanted to establish some kind of relationship with everyone on the team so we could develop a level of trust. I just wanted to get everyone on the same page as soon as possible."

Hammon believes that in basketball the chemistry on the court will follow when there is chemistry among the players off the court. It's important to create a safe environment where players can be themselves and relax. "That combination is possible. Yes, I think the magic formula is time, and I think that's why you get such special relationships when you do spend a great deal of time together," said Hammon. As an example Hammon cited her relationship to teammate Vickie Johnson. She said, "V.J. and I have played seven years together. That's almost two college careers. That's a lot of time invested on the court and off the court, and we do have a special chemistry. I can give her a look both on the court and off the court, and she knows exactly what I am thinking. She knows exactly what I'm going to do, and that just takes time."

However, WNBA basketball is still a business, which Hammon is now well aware of. After all if Babe Ruth can be traded, anyone can be traded. "When it comes down to it, it is a business. Players are sometimes passed along like pieces of meat, so pretty soon they develop a tougher exterior to protect themselves because they know they won't be in one place for every long."

According to Hammon, that translates into a league that is increasingly filled with players who are looking out for themselves. Hammon recalled her first years in the WNBA when she felt more camaraderie between the players. She said, "There was such a sense of camaraderie leaguewide. Everyone was so excited to be playing in her own country. Don't forget, most of these women spend nine months out of the year away from family, friends, and their home country. It was such a tight-knit group. They had this old-school calmness."

Hammon understands that the WNBA is a form of entertainment. As a part of the league, she takes that role seriously. "Keep it in perspective. We are not out there saving lives or sacrificing our lives. We play basketball. We put a ball in a hoop. Think about it. Our sports figures make more money than our president does, and certainly more than the people who are out there fighting for our country," she said.

To Hammon the platform she has as a result of being a professional athlete is a special thing. Being a professional athlete allows Hammon to interact with people at a different level. She said, "I can talk to people, change their entire day by making them smile. I can give them hope and dreams and something to smile and cheer about. Fans pay their hard-earned dollars to come and watch us play. We owe them our best effort every night."

Her former teammate with the Liberty and now teammate in San Antonio, Vickie Johnson recalls when Becky first entered the WNBA. "Becky wasn't drafted, but she came to the Liberty training camp her rookie season with something to prove. She is one of the toughest players that I ever played against and practiced with. Teresa Weatherspoon and I were very hard on her. We'd knock her down, and she'd get right back up again. It just showed us how tough she was."

Hammon recalled her first season in New York as challenging, but those lessons have allowed her to relate to the younger players and with the bench players. "I was in every spot at one point or another. I worked my way all the way up to a starting slot. So I have a real empathy; I know what it's like to want to be on the court and not be able to get out there. You just have to be patient and bide your time. I've always tried to take the higher road, the classy route, always tried to be a professional in every aspect. I have a real appreciation for who is working really hard in practice and who doesn't get the nod on the floor, because I've been there," said Hammon.

Ever since she can remember, she has had a ball in her hands—a basketball, a football, and a softball, a something. For Hammon basketball was a sport she could play by herself. She said, "I had a hoop in my front yard. I'd be out there shooting by myself constantly, playing 'Around the World'. I could just shoot baskets for hours and hours. I always wanted to be better. I can remember coming back from camps or clinics, and my other teammates were enjoying their summer vacations. I was going to the gym. I can remember them asking, 'Aren't you sick of basketball? You just did a whole week of it.' I could never quite relate with that. I just loved to play."

Hammon quickly credits her mom and dad as her primary role models. For her it's the people she's related to as the ones who had the most influence in her life growing up, and her role models haven't changed over the years. She said, "I know my dad and my mom both invested a ton of time, energy, and money in helping me become who I am today. I'm so fortunate to have my parents."

Hammon recalls her father playing with her brother and sister for hours after work. "He played with us for hours after work until it was dark out. We even put floodlights on the court so we could play at night. We'd eat dinner and be right back down there playing again. It was like that for years. And that's where I really learned to play," she recalled.

She realizes how lucky she is to play the game she loves, although unlike many other elite WNBA players she tries not to spend a full winter overseas. She said, "Making money in this lifetime for me is not my number-one priority. It's nice to have some money, be able to play, do the things I want, and to have the things I want. I can always make more money. I can't make more time. I want to be around the people I know and love."

Hammon is also interested in sideline reporting for ESPN. She said, "I'm just trying to establish relationships and improve as a commentator." Hammon cites Doris Burke as a skilled basketball commentator who is one of the best in her profession. While Hammon doesn't think Doris could "hang on the court with her," Hammon laughs as she makes it clear that it's a two-way street. "Doris can't hang with us on the court but throw me in front of a TV camera and I'm the rookie." Hammon hopes to improve her reporting skills and lay some groundwork in the sideline reporting area for ESPN, but that skill set doesn't develop overnight. Hammon said, "If there is someone who knows more, I ask them. You can't be too proud to ask questions."

Yesterday afternoon I picked up the ball and went out to the driveway. It's December, but nearly sixty degrees outside. At the bottom of my driveway, only five or six feet from the Hudson River, a weathered basketball hoop is affixed to an old potting shed. The driveway slants slightly downward from left to right, and a rock wall cuts off most of the right side of the court. I shot around for maybe twenty minutes. I felt the breeze off the Hudson River mingle with the tears streaming down my face. This was the first time I had actually picked up a basketball in many months, although I had been watching basketball daily, picking games and players apart, preaching x's and o's, both as a high-school assistant coach and as a writer. I'd been studying stats and watching other players warm up night after night. This was the first time in a long while that the leather slid through my hands and not someone else's. It felt good.

Afterward I sat facing the Hudson River for several minutes quietly contemplating the beauty of the game and the level at which I still enjoy and love it. It felt right. I felt at home in my driveway hoop with its uneven surface and mildewed backboard with the square worn off. I felt more at home listening to the way my basketball sounded on the pavement and on the metal hoop than I had felt in many months of sitting in Madison Square Garden and countless other arenas or high-school gyms watching other women and young girls do what I still dream and yearn to do.

I often wonder what kind of player I would have been in the WNBA. Rather than articulate it and ruin it with words, I'd much rather close my eyes and imagine myself as the player I always dreamed I could be. I often wonder why we are told to stop daydreaming as we get older. Daydreams keep us sane and remind us that it's OK to look beyond the present we find ourselves in. Sometimes daydreams give us hope when hope is a tall order.

The truth of the matter is that as we pass through life, we do have regrets. Some of them slide away into the recesses of our memories; some stay fixed and clinging like ivy on a rock wall. I can't imagine basketball not being a part of this story, of my story. It is the framework of my world. It is my foundation, my haven, my glory days, and my most profound heartbreak.

We all experience loss. We are all disappointed by life one way or another. We all go on. The game of basketball is about the pursuit of perfection and the fleeting moments when that perfection actually illuminates itself. Anyone who has ever really played the game understands that at some point in their formative years, they were hard-wired to sweat, hurt, and chase perfection, rarely if ever to catch it. Most will find regret and loss much more often than wins and the celebrations.

My friend and editor at *Full Court Press*, Clay Kallam, recently wrote, "Losing is part of the bargain, part of the game, part of what makes sports so attractive. In an ambiguous world, athletics offers the black and the white, the W and the L, no matter how close or hotly contested. At game's end, someone wins and someone loses. Judgment of a sort has occurred, a judgment we seek when we start the process. After all, if we didn't want to know where we stood, we wouldn't play the game in the first place."[1]

At night I dream of long conversations with players on WNBA

teams—conversations held on the basketball court, sometimes with words and sometimes without. In one dream I spoke with San Antonio's starting point guard, Becky Hammon. In this dream, I had somehow hurt my hand in a drill, and it was bleeding. Hammon saw the blood and looked queasy. I laughed and asked if a little blood could actually make her sick. She told me she hated the sight of blood but that I should play in the WNBA and then I would experience all kinds of pain.

I replied, "There is pain away from the game too. Some of us are given the heart and the talent to play while others are just given the heart." In my dream we were standing very close, my blood dripping on the shiny hardwood like it has done so many other times before, but when I looked down to see how much blood I had lost, it was gone, sucked into the hardwood like so much else I left on the court over the years.

Some things never change, I thought, as I found a broom to clear my playing area off, out of habit more than anything else. The rituals and routines of playing on and maintaining a driveway basketball court dictated the seasons of my youth. In the spring I cleaned the debris and painstakingly repainted the foul line and three-point lines. In the summer I hosed the court down to keep the pavement cool. In the fall I swept off the acorns and fallen oak leaves from the court. In the winter I shoveled the snow. My seasons were measured by the amount of work I did to prepare my playing surface. As I swept I realized that I was no longer left with only my daydreams of last-second shots and perfect passes and crossover dribbles. I began this journey tired of a career away from sports, empty inside because I was not doing what I was meant to do. A master's degree, thousands of reward air miles and countless articles later, I'm right back where I started, dribbling a basketball on the uneven pavement, relishing the sound of a chain net and a ball.

Game after game I watch players go through the exact same routine prior to the tipoff. All players have unique superstitions and odd routines that help them mentally prepare for the game ahead. Among all the most bizarre individual superstitions, there is one universal, unspoken rule of the court. You never walk off in warm-ups or in practice without hitting your final shot. It doesn't matter if it's a lay-up or a twenty-two-foot jumper. If you miss, you keep shooting until you make it.

Shooting around in my driveway, I recalled a conversation I had once with Hammon. She explained deep-rooted passion for the game: "Everyone has their moments trying to stay motivated, but for the most part, I get up and go play because I like to. People are sometimes afraid of hard work. I've never been one to shy away from hard work; it doesn't scare me in the least to work hard—I was always a gym rat growing up—I never really looked at it as work. I love challenging myself."

In reality the fans really see the final product. They don't see everything else that goes into it. The years, the hours of sweat, the hard work. Hammon is frequently asked how she became such a good player. Her answer is always the same: "I played it. All the time."

"The great thing about basketball is you can't buy your way into being good. You can only work your way up. It's the purest thing. There is nothing you can do other than dedicate yourself to becoming as good as you're supposed to be, as good as you want to be," said Hammon. Of course Hammon wants to improve her game. "Until you shoot 100 percent from everywhere, there is always room for improvement," she said.

"I remember the times by myself in the gym: just me, the ball, and the hoop. There's serenity in those moments. It's a place where I can just relax and be myself. It's my place of peace," Hammon said.

Sitting on the banks of the Hudson River, I understood at last, that the basketball court is my place of peace too. A player is a player; we're not so different from one another after all. Young girls in grade school, high school, and NCAA athletes, the elite basketball players of the WNBA and USA Basketball, both past and present, all play one game. We play, finally, because we can.

Epilogue Building the Perfect Player

I n every interview I asked players and coaches one standard
question: If you could build or create the perfect basketball
player, what skills or mindset would she possess?
Here are their answers.

Mike McManus, *Former Head Coach, St. Thomas Aquinas College*

I believe every player must be able to handle the basketball. Every player needs to shoot the ball from the outside. Even guards need to know what to do in the post. A player like Diana Taurasi is a perfect example because she can play any position on the floor. Every player must know how, and be willing, to play defense. Every player needs to get up on someone whether they have the ball or they don't have the ball.

If you can handle and pass the ball, a coach is going to notice it. The player who can handle the ball and not wilt under pressure, that's the kid I want on my team.

Dan Hughes, *Head Coach, San Antonio Silver Stars*

Vickie Johnson has a lot of what I would like. I love the players who have that competitive greatness, who understand when the game is very important and are willing to make the right basketball play. They don't always go to their individual strength and just rely on that; they may use that as a pathway; they make good basketball decisions. Vickie Johnson, Dawn Staley, and Suzie McConnell-Serio all had that. Those players were very good at crucial times playing the game in a mature way.

I love really persistent personalities. I love people who think in terms of giving one more effort, get us the ball one more time and we'll make something happen, but I really appreciate those players who will make the right basketball play. I can put the ball in their hands because I know that if they get doubled, the correct pass will be made. If they're not doubled, they have the courage to make that play. It's a rare commodity when a player has that competitive greatness, and they want to be at their best at key times.

James Anderson, *Former Head Coach, Narbonne High School*

Skills—dribbling first. It's a hard skill to teach. Then probably shooting. If you're a great dribbler, you're usually a pretty good passer and scorer because no one is going to stop you from getting where you want to get.

Mindset—the first thing is to be unselfish. I tell my athletes, "Don't be selfish, be selfless." If you lose a game, look in the mirror and just say you know, it was my fault. Don't try anything else.

I always tell people the one thing you can't teach is heart. You can't make somebody competitive. That's the one thing I've learned. You can make kids play harder, but certain kids just aren't going to be competitive.

You look at a kid like Diana Taurasi. I played against her in high school. She's not a great defender, but she knows where to be. I don't think I played against a kid who was more competitive than her. She is not the most physically gifted kid, but she knows how to do things because her basketball IQ is just off the chart.

Christina Wielgus, *Head Coach, Dartmouth College*

Obviously inherent athleticism because you can't teach it. The second thing would be vision. You have to have court vision. The best players are the ones who understand the pass to the assist to the shot. I do think that the ability to score is important. We can teach defense. Coaches are good at teaching defense. Offense requires an enormous amount of repetition, and most coaches just skim over that.

Clearly the ability to score. I don't mean scoring every possible shot, but there are certain fundamental shots you have to hit.

As a coach, everyone wants to know your plays. They all think that its plays that will win games. You know what the end of a game situation requires of me? I tell them which player should have the ball. We have movement. I put the ball in someone's hands. The best player can think, "I'll take the shot if I have it, but if I don't, I'll dump it here, and they can make that play."

There are two types of players you need on your team to win a championship. The first kind is a player that wins a game for you, and the second kind is the one who won't lose it. There are so many players that think that they can win the game, but they can't. And they start chucking up shots and doing stupid things. If they could just stay in good defensive stance, get the ball to the better player, and keep moving. You have to know whether you are the go-to player or the role player.

Dianne Nolan, *Assistant Coach, Yale University;*
Former Head Coach, Fairfield University

Players now are faster and stronger. I always look for speed. Good hands. A vision of what plays should look like. Six-foot [laughs]. Competitive, compassionate, and hardworking. I feel there is more of an entitlement feeling. We were raised as Title IX babies, that you got things by working hard. Right now I think the current players sometimes don't understand how necessary a hard-work ethic really is, that you really have to work hard to get what you want. Team sports mean that you sacrifice your individuality for the team.

Janice Quinn, *Head Coach, New York University*

I'm always going to go with athleticism. I think the perfect player for me is first and foremost a great athlete with quickness, with agility, with coordination, with lateral speed. Because the way we like to play, the way I like to coach, is wide open. I don't like to pigeonhole the players into little boxes. I like them to paint free form.

Good size, good speed, good coordination, you have to start with that. The other ingredients are a love of the actual basketball game itself because that means they have an unlimited potential. Seventy-five percent of the kids playing this game don't love it. They don't really truly, truly love the game itself—the physics, the geometry of the game. There is so much in it. Too many young athletes have no willingness to master the game. They want to play it for social reasons, maybe for ego reasons, but not because they love it.

Becky Hammon, *San Antonio Silver Stars*

You definitely need some God-given talent, but from there, it's in your court. I've seen players with a talent level a five out of ten fulfill their expectations, but I also see players who have a talent level of ten out of ten only play 50 percent. So who is getting the most out of their potential?

Crystal Robison, *Assistant Coach, Washington Mystics*

I don't think just anybody can say, "I want to be a professional athlete, I want to be a basketball player." You have to have some gifts. Most of the people that get to this level love the game and have physical talent. Not everyone can play at this level even if they really want to. It has to be something that's in you. The amount of work you have to put in is unbelievable. I've seen so many talented players not make it because they were not taught the right way. I think that's the key: young girls need to have coaches who will teach them the right things so that they can progress every year and at every level.

Don't give up on your dreams and work hard. Be ready to sacrifice. Because to get to this level, you definitely make a lot of sacrifices. We don't see our families a lot, we're always traveling, we're always in the gym. We miss out on all the parties and those kinds of things. Be ready and be willing to make sacrifices to achieve this because you have to be willing to sacrifice things in order to make something of your life.

Nancy Lieberman, *Hall of Famer and Analyst*

She would be Candace Parker. She would be She-bron. Parker has the physical tools: she's six feet four, she's long, athletic. She's mentally tough. She has passion. You have to have passion and be competitive and want to compete all the time. You must have Michael Jordan's mindset, be able to play multiple positions, and be excited to get after it defensively. Defense is about pride. It's more me against you and I'm going win. I'm going to stop you. It's a mentality. Those are the things to me that the complete player must have: the mental, the physical, the versatility. Be fortunate enough to have the physical characteristics but also possess that multidimensional skill set and just want to win. Because I don't just want to play, I want to win.

Jody Conradt, *Former Head Coach, University of Texas*

A player who makes everyone on the floor better. A player who is selfless and understands her individual role and can be depended on to execute within that role. A player who is super competitive, super talented, an extraordinary athlete.

I'd like to say you can teach certain qualities like motivation, intensity, teamwork, but I don't think we have research to substantiate it. Instead we can only say that we create an environment that enhances. We create the lab where those skills can be practiced.

There is a competitive spirit in all of us to varying degrees, and people who have those intangible qualities find a way to express it.

Gail Goestenkors, *Head Coach, University of Texas;*
Assistant Coach, USA Basketball

She would have a quiet confidence about her. She would have a lot of grit and determination to be the very best. She would have a mental and physical toughness. She gets knocked down, she's going to come right back at you. She would uplift others. She would not just be a great player, but she would elevate her teammates to a higher level, and to her community.

Skillwise, she would have great athleticism. She'd be quick, good speed, ball handling ability, passing ability. We can always improve our shooters, so that's not at the top of the list. Have a great desire to be a tremendous defensive player. So much of what we do is predicated upon our defense and that's more desire than anything else.

Appendix A
High School
Participation
by State

STATE	SCHOOLS	PARTICIPATION
Alabama	409	5,492
Alaska	108	1,715
Arizona	224	6,292
Arkansas	238	4,217
California	1,207	33,596
Colorado	315	7,923
Connecticut	174	4,162
Delaware	49	615
District of Columbia	15	218
Florida	581	10,998
Georgia	374	9,171
Hawaii	64	1,585
Idaho	145	3,628
Illinois	662	17,871
Indiana	383	10,316
Iowa	397	8,934
Kansas	360	7,975
Kentucky	268	6,113
Louisiana	397	9,925
Maine	141	3,509
Maryland	184	4,678
Massachusetts	340	10,396
Michigan	720	20,541
Minnesota	454	13,229
Mississippi	257	6,307
Missouri	535	12,432
Montana	182	3,433
Nebraska	314	7,172
Nevada	92	2,439
New Hampshire	87	2,228
New Jersey	405	10,150
New York	688	17,850
North Carolina	352	8,032
North Dakota	179	2,777
Ohio	800	18,388
Oklahoma	471	7,600
Oregon	286	6,580
Pennsylvania	692	20,760
Rhode Island	48	1,170
South Carolina	196	5,049
South Dakota	171	3,072
Tennessee	362	6,621
Texas	1,222	70,232
Utah	118	2,807
Vermont	68	1,692
Virginia	294	7,896
Washington	325	8,663
West Virginia	135	2,122
Wisconsin	477	12,943
Wyoming	68	1,611

Source: National Federation of State High School Associations, 2004–2005
NFHA *High School Athletics Participation Survey 2005* (Indianapolis IN: National
Federation of State High School Associations, 2005).

Appendix B The Structure of USA Basketball

The following information is supplied by USA Basketball. The author appreciates the continued support and assistance from USA Basketball with regard to this project.

USA Basketball is an organization composed of associations. Current USA Basketball active members include the Amateur Athletic Union (AAU); Continental Basketball Association (CBA); National Association of Basketball Coaches (NABC); National Association of Intercollegiate Athletics (NAIA); National Basketball Association (NBA); National Basketball Association Development League; National Collegiate Athletic Association (NCAA); National Federation of State High School Associations (NFHS); National Junior College Athletic Association (NJCAA); National Pro-Am City League

Association (NPACLA); National Wheelchair Basketball Association (NWBA); United States Armed Forces; USA Deaf Sports Federation (USADSF); Women's Basketball Coaches Association (WBCA); and the Women's National Basketball Association (WNBA). The fifteen-member organizations have representation on USA Basketball's board of directors and various committees and ultimately determine how USA Basketball operates. The various committees for USA Basketball not only make a significant number of policy decisions for the organization but also select athletes and coaches for the various teams fielded.

According to USA Basketball, women's basketball became a medal sport at the 1976 Olympics. USA teams don't just compete in the Olympic Games. They also regularly compete in the World Championships, Pan American Games, World University Games, men's and women's U21 World Championships, men's and women's U19 World Championships, Hoop Summit, and USA Basketball Youth Development Festivals. USA Basketball also sanctions U.S. basketball team tours of foreign countries and foreign basketball team tours of the United States, as well as overseeing the certification of FIBA and USA Basketball officials and the assignment of those officials to international competitions and the licensing of players to play professionally overseas.

The following events make up the various sanctioned events that USA Basketball regularly competes in as described by USA Basketball:

Olympic Games

Men's and women's Olympic basketball competition is held every four years (2008, 2012, etc.). The USA women have earned the gold in five of the past six Olympics and overall boast of a sterling 42-3 record. Beijing, China, is the site of the 2008 Games.

FIBA World Championships

Men's and women's competition is held every four years at the FIBA World Championships (2006, 2010, etc.). Unlike the Olympics in which twelve teams participate, twenty-four countries compete in the World Championship for Men and sixteen teams participate in the World Championship for Women. In basketball circles, the World Championship title is considered as prestigious as the Olympic title. The USA women successfully defended the gold medal after finishing a perfect 9-0 in China in 2002. In 2006 the USA women captured the bronze medal with an 8-1 record.

Under 21 FIBA World Championships

In 2003 FIBA initiated a Women's U21 World Championship and the USA women claimed the gold, finishing 7-1 in Sibenik, Croatia. The next FIBA U21 World Championship for women is scheduled for 2007. The selections of the players and coaches are made by the USA Basketball Collegiate Committees.

Pan American Games

Started in 1955 for women, the Pan American Games are held every four years (2007, 2011, etc.) in the year preceding the Olympics. Only countries from FIBA America are eligible to compete. The USA women have won six of twelve gold medals and rolled up a 67-12 record.

World University Games

The World University Games are held for women every two years (2007, 2009, etc.); only current university student athletes or recent graduates are eligible.

Under 19 World Championships/Junior National Teams

USA Basketball also fields women's national teams for players nineteen years old or younger. FIBA holds U19 World Championships every two years. USA Basketball also fields teams featuring players eighteen years old or younger for FIBA Americas Zone qualifying tournaments. The selections of the players and coaches are made by the USA Basketball Collegiate Committees.

Hoop Summit

The Hoop Summit is the country's premiere annual basketball game featuring America's top senior boy high-school players taking on a World Select Team composed of the world's top players nineteen years old or younger and are played each April.

USA Basketball Youth Development Festivals

Held annually each June since 2002 for women, USA Basketball's Youth Development Festival is an entry-level event that combines competition with off-court educational seminars. Featuring three USA teams composed of top players who are high-school juniors or sophomores from around the United States, the festival in 2005 for the first time featured international teams. Festival coaches are top high-school and AAU coaches. The selections of the players and coaches are made by the USA Basketball Junior Development Committees.

Notes

1. Heck Yeah, I'm a Tomboy!

1. Mike May, *Sports Participation in America* (Washington DC: Sporting Goods Manufacturers Association, 2003).
2. L. K. Bunker, "Life-Long Benefits of Youth Sport Participation for Girls and Women" (lecture, Sport Psychology Conference, University of Virginia, Charlottesville, June 22, 1988).
3. Sporting Goods Manufacturers Association, *Gaining Ground* (Washington DC: Sporting Goods Manufacturers Association, 2000).
4. Women's Sports Foundation, *The Women's Sports Foundation Report: Her Life Depends on It: Sport, Physical Activity and the Health and Well-Being of American Girls* (East Meadow NY: Women's Sports Foundation, 2004).

2. The Fun Factor

1. George Sheehan, "Playing," in *Sport and Religion*, ed. Shirl J. Hoffman, 83–87 (Chicago: Human Kinetics Books, 1992).

2. Dawn Staley, blog entry, *The Official Home Page of the Houston Comets*, http://www.wnba.com/comets (accessed August 22, 2006).

3. Ryan Hedstrom and Daniel Gould, *Research in Youth Sports: Critical Issues Status* (East Lansing: Michigan State University, 2004), 9.

3. You Can't Measure Heart

1. National Federation of State High School Associations, 2004–2005 NFHA *High School Athletics Participation Survey 2005* (Indianapolis IN: National Federation of State High School Associations, 2005).

2. National Federation of State High School Associations, 2004–2005 NFHA *High School Athletics.*

3. R. Acosta and L. Carpenter, "Women in Intercollegiate Sport: A Longitudinal Study—Nineteen Year Update, 1977–1996" (unpublished manuscript, Brooklyn College, 1996); and National Federation of State High School Associations, 2004–2005 NFHA *High School Athletics.*

4. National Federation of State High School Associations, *The Case for High School Activities* (Indianapolis IN: National Federation of State High School Associations, 2005).

5. National Federation of State High School Associations, *The Case for High School Activities.*

6. National Federation of State High School Associations, *The Case for High School Activities.*

4. The Crème of the Crop

1. Courtesy of Christ the King High School.

2. Courtesy of the AAU.

5. Three Divisions, One Association

1. NCAA, "Our Mission," *National Collegiate Athletic Association*, http://www.NCAA.org.

2. NCAA, "Membership," *National Collegiate Athletic Association*, http://www.NCAA.org.

3. NCAA, "History of NCAA," *National Collegiate Athletic Association*, http://www.NCAA.org.

4. NCAA, 1981–82–2004–05 NCAA *Sports Sponsorship and Participation Rates Report* (Indianapolis IN: NCAA, 2005).

5. NCAA, 1981–82–2004–05 NCAA *Sports Sponsorship and Participation Rates Report.*

6. Acosta and Carpenter, "Women in Intercollegiate Sport."

7. Courtesy of Fairfield University Athletics.

8. Courtesy of Fairfield University Athletics.

9. Courtesy of Fairfield University Athletics.

6. Conradt, Goestenkors, and the Pursuit

1. Courtesy of University of Texas Athletics.
2. Courtesy of University of Texas Athletics.
3. Courtesy of University of Texas Athletics.

7. The Approach of a Coach

1. Courtesy of Dartmouth University Athletics.
2. Courtesy of Dartmouth University Athletics.
3. Courtesy of New York University Athletics.
4. Courtesy of New York University Athletics.

9. Over Ten Years and Going Strong

1. Clay Kallam, "The WNBA at Age 10," *Full Court Press*, May 3, 1997, http://www.fullcourt.com.
2. Kallam, "The WNBA at Age 10."
3. Richard Lapchick, *Race and Gender Report Card: The Women's National Basketball Association* (Orlando: University of Central Florida Institute for Diversity and Ethics in Sport, 2005).
4. Scott Salinardi, "She's Got Game: Women's Interest in Sports Grows Significantly," *Media and Entertainment Trend Report*, February 2004.
5. Salinardi, "She's Got Game."
6. *Sports Business Journal*, December 24–30, 2001.
7. Harris Poll Online, poll #16, by Humphrey Taylor, March 10, 1999.
8. Leslie Heywood and Shari Dworkin, *Built to Win: The Female Athlete as Cultural Icon* (Minneapolis: University of Minnesota Press, 2003).
9. Jane McManus, "Not Many View Women's Sports as Must-See TV," *White Plains (NY) Journal News*, December 11, 2005.
10. Salinardi, "She's Got Game."
11. Courtesy of the San Antonio Silver Stars and the WNBA.

11. The United States versus the Rest

1. Shirl S. Hoffman, ed., *Sport and Religion* (Champaign IL: Human Kinetics Books, 1992).
2. Courtesy of USA Basketball.
3. Clay Kallam, "Youth Development Festival Impressions," *Full Court Press*, July 19, 2007, http://www.fullcourt.com.
4. Denise Lardner Carmody, "Big-Time Spectator Sports: A Feminist Christian Perspective," in *Sport and Religion*, ed. Shirl J. Hoffman, 105–10 (Champaign IL: Human Kinetics Publishers, 1992).
5. Courtesy of USA Basketball.

12. The Best in the World

1. Courtesy of USA Basketball.
2. Courtesy of Temple University Athletics.

13. The Slippery Slope of Gender Politics

1. David F. Salter, *Crashing the Old Boys' Network: The Tragedies and Triumphs of Girls and Women in Sports* (Westport CT: Praeger Publishing, 1996).
2. Salter, *Crashing the Old Boys' Network*.
3. Salter, *Crashing the Old Boys' Network*.
4. Amanda Smith, "Back-Page Bylines: Newspapers, Women and Sport," in *SportCult*, ed. Randy Martin and Toby Miller, 253–61 (Minneapolis: University of Minnesota Press, 1999).
5. Margaret Carlisle Duncan and Michael Messner, *Gender in Televised Sports: News and Highlights Shows, 1989–2004* (Los Angeles: Amateur Athletic Foundation of Los Angeles, 1991).
6. Michael A. Messner, *Taking the Field: Women, Men, and Sports* (Minneapolis: University of Minnesota Press, 2002).
7. E. J. Staurowsky, "Women and Men in the Press Box: The Price of Progress" (Ithaca NY: Ithaca College, 2002).
8. Duncan and Messner, *Gender in Televised Sports*.

14. Unique but Alike

1. Special thanks to RLR Associates Limited for Burke's background information. http://www.rlrassociates.com.
2. Nancy Lieberman's biography furnished courtesy of www.nancy lieberman.com. http://www.nancylieberman.com/biography.asp.

15. Her Place of Peace

1. Lieberman biography, http://www.nancylieberman.com/biography.asp.

Suggested Reading

Acosta, R., and L. Carpenter. "Women in Intercollegiate Sport: A Longitudinal Study—Nineteen Year Update, 1977–1996." Unpublished manuscript, Brooklyn College, 1996.

Bolin, Anne, and Jane Granskog, eds. *Athletic Intruders: Ethnographic Research on Women, Culture, and Exercise.* Albany: State University of New York Press, 2003.

Duncan, Margaret Carlisle, and Michael Messner. *Coverage of Women's Sports in Four Daily Newspapers.* Los Angeles: Amateur Athletic Foundation of Los Angeles, 2005.

———. *Gender in Televised Sports: News and Highlights Shows, 1989–2004.* Los Angeles: Amateur Athletic Foundation of Los Angeles, 1991.

Heywood, Leslie, and Shari Dworkin. *Built to Win: The Female Athlete as Cultural Icon.* Minneapolis: University of Minnesota Press, 2003.

Hoffman, Shirl S., ed. *Sport and Religion.* Champaign IL: Human Kinetics Books, 1992.

Hult, Joan S., and Marianna Trekell. *A Century of Women's Basketball: From Frailty to Final Four*. Reston VA: National Association for Girls and Women in Sport, 1991.

Kane, Mary Jo. "Media Coverage of the Post Title IX Female Athlete—A Feminist Analysis of Sport, Gender and Power." *Duke Journal of Gender Law and Policy* 3 (1996): 95–127.

Lannin, Joanne. *A History of Basketball for Girls and Women: From Bloomers to Big Leagues*. Minneapolis: Lerner Sports, 2000.

Macy, Sue. *Play Like a Girl: A Celebration of Women in Sports*. New York: Henry Holt, 1999.

May, Mike. *Sports Participation in America*. Washington DC: Sporting Goods Manufacturers Association, 2003.

McManus, Jane. "Not Many View Women's Sports as Must-See TV." *White Plains (NY) Journal News*, December 11, 2005.

Messner, Michael A. *Taking the Field: Women, Men, and Sports*. Minneapolis: University of Minnesota Press, 2002.

Mumford, Vincent E. "A Look at Women's Participation in Sports in Maryland Two-Year Colleges." *Sport Journal* 8, no. 1 (Winter 2005). http://www.thesportjournal.org/article/look-womens-participation-sports-maryland-two-year-colleges.

Pemberton, Cynthia Lee A. *More Than a Game: One Woman's Fight for Gender Equity in Sport*. Boston: Northeastern University Press, 2002.

Rarg Bill, Marlene. *Winning Women in Basketball*. Hauppauge NY: Barron's, 2000.

Salinardi, Scott. "She's Got Game: Women's Interest in Sports Grows Significantly." *Media and Entertainment Trend Report*, February 2004.

Salter, David F. *Crashing the Old Boys' Network: The Tragedies and Triumphs of Girls and Women in Sports*. Westport CT: Praeger Publishing, 1996.

Sandoz, Joli. *Whatever It Takes: Women on Women's Sports*. New York: Farrar, Straus and Giroux, 1999.

Smith, Amanda. "Back-Page Bylines: Newspapers, Women and Sport." In *SportCult*, edited by Randy Martin and Toby Miller, 253–61. Minneapolis: University of Minneapolis Press, 1999.

Smith, Lissa. *Nike Is a Goddess: The History of Women in Sports*. New York: Atlantic Monthly Press, 1999.

Staurowsky, E. J. "Women and Men in the Press Box: The Price of Progress." Ithaca NY: Ithaca College, 2002.

Breinigsville, PA USA
20 March 2011
257981BV00002B/2/P